ALL THE BEST PASTA SAUCES

Cookbooks by Joie Warner

ALL THE BEST PASTA SAUCES
ALL THE BEST SALADS
ALL THE BEST PIZZAS
ALL THE BEST CHICKEN DINNERS
ALL THE BEST MEXICAN MEALS
ALL THE BEST MUFFINS AND QUICK BREADS
ALL THE BEST POTATOES
ALL THE BEST COOKIES
ALL THE BEST PASTA SAUCES II
ALL THE BEST RICE
THE COMPLETE BOOK OF CHICKEN WINGS
THE BRAUN HAND BLENDER COOKBOOK
A TASTE OF CHINATOWN
JOIE WARNER'S SPAGHETTI
JOIE WARNER'S CAESAR SALADS
JOIE WARNER'S APPLE DESERTS

ALL THE BEST PASTA SAUCES

BY

JOIE WARNER

HEARST BOOKS • New York

A FLAVOR BOOK

Recognizing the importance of preserving what has been written, it is the policy of William Morrow and Company, Inc., and its imprints and affiliates to have the books it publishes printed on acid-free paper, and we exert our best efforts to that end.

LIBRARY OF CONGRESS CATALOGING-IN-PUBLICATION DATA
Warner, Joie
All the best pasta sauces/by Joie Warner.
p. cm.
Includes index.
ISBN 0-688-10127-5
1. Sauces 2. Cookery (Pasta) I. Title. II. Title: Pasta sauces.
TX819.A1W37 1991
641.8'22-dc20 90-42480
CIP

Printed in the United States of America
8 9 10

This book was created and produced by

Flavor Publications, Inc.
208 East 51st Street, Suite 240
New York, New York 10022

ACKNOWLEDGMENTS

THANKS TO: My husband and partner, Drew, for his superb and imaginative design; his production expertise; and for eating pasta for breakfast, lunch, and dinner for many months without too much complaining!

My friend Kristina Goodwin of Savouries Catering for generously sharing her wonderful recipes: Creamy Sun-Dried Tomato Sauce; Oyster Mushroom Sauce; Chicken Artichoke Sauce; Sweetbreads and Tomato Sauce; and Fusilli with Seafood in Lemon Vinaigrette – and for helping me test and create some of the sauces.

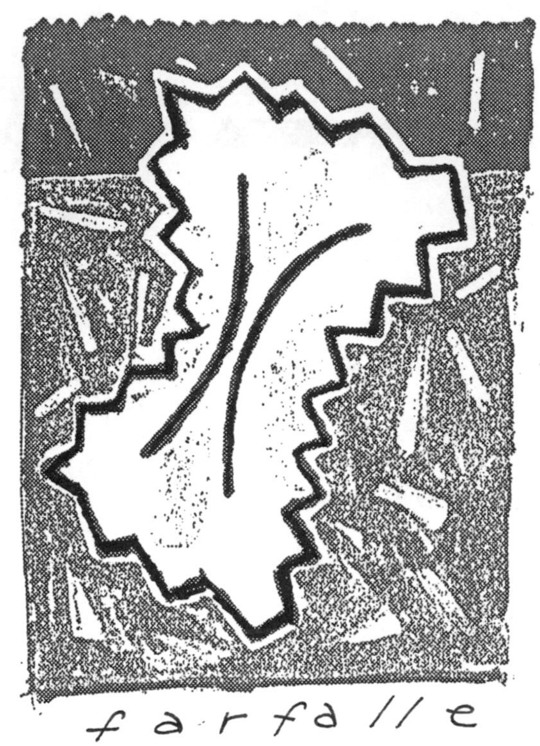
farfalle

INTRODUCTION

PASTA needs little introduction to Americans; in fact, in the past few years we have become utterly pasta crazy. Because of our insatiable appetites for light, fresh, easy food that can be served with panache, we have been gobbling up more and more of this agreeable starch every year.

It is hard to imagine that until quite recently pasta in America meant either spaghetti with tomato sauce or macaroni and cheese. Nowadays, cooks of all persuasions have begun to discover not only the dozens of fanciful shapes and sizes, but the rainbow of colors of both freshly made and dried pastas, along with the dazzling variety of fresh and flavorful sauces that accompany them.

Au courant chefs and restaurants were the first to inspire our pasta mania. They thrilled our taste buds (while at the same time charging exorbitant prices) by serving us pasta made with top quality and recherché ingredients presented with pizzazz. American chefs, in their quest for new culinary ideas, explored pasta's possibilities and proved along the way that pasta had no need to be traditional — that it readily lent itself to creativity and innovation.

Indeed, pasta has swiftly become the food of the '90s — a wholesome staple in everyone's diet. Its popularity and universal appeal is due to the fact that pasta is one of the most satisfying, versatile foods ever created. It tastes wonderful prepared in myriad ways, and can be served hot, cold, or at room temperature. It's economical. And, once and for all, forget the notion that pasta is fattening - it's low-cal and low-fat, as long as it is sauced lightly. You can avoid cream or butter sauces if you are concerned with saturated fats. Choose instead sauces using olive oil, which has been shown to actually lower cholesterol levels because it is high in monounsaturates. (My philosophy regarding dieting is to eat what you like, just don't eat too much of it!) In addition, pasta contains complex carbohydrates, providing as much energy as pure protein, and, moreover, it gives you a feeling of satiety long after you have eaten — a definite boon for the weight conscious. In short, pasta is healthy. Pasta is good for you!

To most gastronomes, the noodle is the superstar, not the sauce. But as Jack Denton Scott says in his classic cookbook, *The Complete Book of Pasta*, "without an interesting sauce, one with a subtle, different flavor, pasta is simply a bland dish of spaghetti or what have you."

All The Best Pasta Sauces is a celebration of that interesting sauce — the sauces that turn a bland dish of cooked dough into something wonderful. I believe this is the first cookbook devoted to the panoply of inventive pasta sauces that range from the simple to the truly sophisticated, although this collection only skims the surface of the culinary possibilities. Here you will find zesty, colorful sauces for first courses, entrées, and side dishes eminently suited to any occasion from the casual to the elegant. Most are Italian in origin, many are Italian in inspiration, with some sauces from other parts of Europe and the Far East. Many are classics with my own flourishes; others are my renditions of sauces I have enjoyed in restaurants. All told, I have cooked and tested hundreds of recipes for this book and selected my favorites — sauces that I consider to be best of the best, all the while trying to present as broad a range of flavors as possible.

All The Best Pasta Sauces is organized by type of sauce rather than type of noodle, with recommendations on what pasta to pair each sauce with. Most of the recipes suggest using dried pastas because these are still the most readily available. If you live near a shop or supermarket that sells fresh pasta, or if you have time to make your own on occasion, then you have the best of both worlds. Pasta is one of the most democratic foods, which means that ultimately, you can mix and match most sauces with any type of pasta you wish.

You will find the sauces in this book very easy and quick to cook. Contrary to popular belief, "long cooked" sauces – in particular tomato sauces – do not have to cook for hours and hours (with the exception of ragus). Long cooking actually tends to turn a tomato sauce bitter and acidic, while short cooking retains the flavor and color of the ingredients in virtually any sauce. That is why my favorite sauces cook in less time than it takes to boil the water or cook the pasta; they will inevitably be lighter and fresher tasting.

Sauces for pasta can be improvised at will, too. There are hundreds of combinations of ingredients and seasonings which complement a simple dish of noodles – the variety is limited only by the imagination. It is so easy to try out different flavors, to invent your own sauces, and if you do not have the exact ingredients for a particular recipe, it is often easy to substitute something else. Above all, feel free to experiment.

I prefer sauces that are uncomplicated and intensely flavored. I use some seasonings – especially garlic and black pepper – with abandon. If your preference is for subtle, delicate flavors, just reduce the garlic or other seasonings accordingly. But I urge you to try it my way first! By relying on the seasonings to flavor a sauce, my recipes do not call for much salt: I prefer to allow guests to add salt at the table if they wish.

The secret to making good sauces is simple. Begin with the best ingredients. Use the freshest produce, the best olive oils, cheeses, and specialty items such as imported black olives and sun-dried tomatoes. Find a reliable fishmonger, butcher, and cheese store, and be demanding. Encourage shop owners to carry specialty items or products you may require. And pair your sauce with quality fresh or dried pasta.

JOIE WARNER

BASICS

TYPES OF PASTA AND HOW TO BUY IT

ITALIAN AND DOMESTIC When buying pasta, quality comes first. Although the different brands may appear alike, they will not taste the same. The two types of pasta – dried and fresh – come in countless varieties. And contrary to all the recent hoopla, fresh pasta is not superior to dried. They are equally delicious, each with its own taste and texture, and they are usually paired with different sauces.

The best dried pasta is made from durum (hard) wheat that has been ground into semolina, and water. All Italian dried pasta and most American brands are made with this preferred wheat which contains more proteins and vitamins than regular flour. The dough is mixed, kneaded, stretched, and extruded or stamped out to form the desired shape, then dried. Spaghetti, macaroni, and rigatoni are the most familiar pastas in this category. Some American manufacturers use a combination of semolina and common flours, producing a pasta which can be acceptable if cooked properly but is also very easily overcooked (it takes less time than pasta made with semolina only). Pasta made with 100 percent durum semolina takes a few minutes longer to cook, yet is more resilient than other types. Good pasta has a subtle, nutty taste and chewy texture all its own. That is why in Italy, pasta is appreciated in its own right and not just as a vehicle for the sauce.

There are over 100 names for the wide variety of shapes, sizes, thicknesses, and textures of Italian dried pastas, which can be very confusing. Not only that, but the names change from region to region. The following chart lists the most common dried pasta varieties available in America.

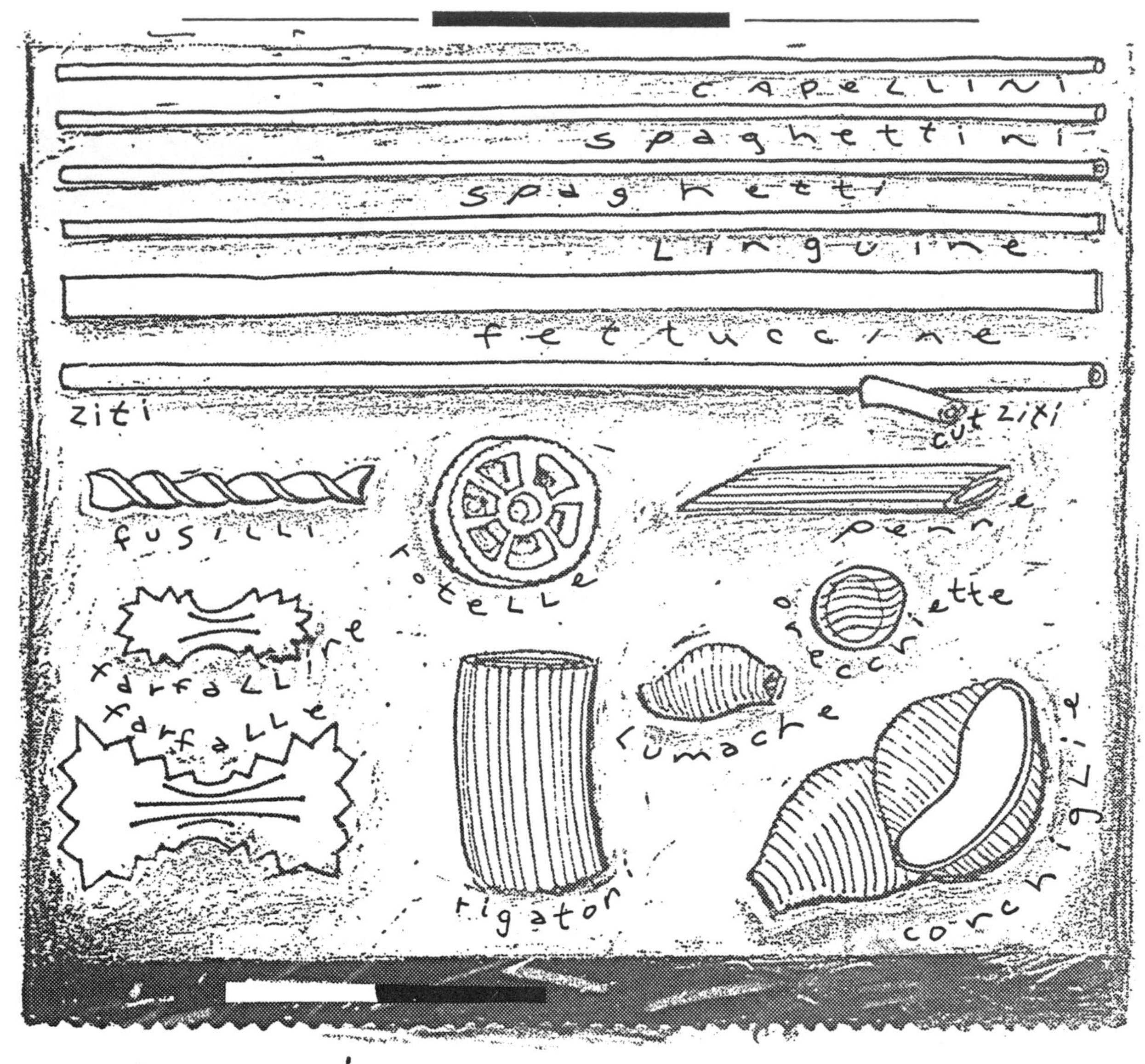

capellini
spaghettini
spaghetti
linguine
fettuccine
ziti
cut ziti
fusilli
rotelle
penne
farfalline
farfalle
orecchiette
lumache
rigatoni
conchiglie

dried pasta

A great resource, dried pasta can be stored in a dry cupboard almost indefinitely in its unopened package or a sealed container.

The widest variety of imported dried pasta can be found in Italian grocery stores or specialty food shops. In many large communities, supermarkets also carry a good selection of both domestic and Italian brands.

SPECIALTY PASTA Other dried varieties are made from Jerusalem artichoke flour, buckwheat flour, soy flour (high protein flour), and whole wheat flour. These can usually be found in health food stores and some supermarkets. They have a unique taste and texture all their own.

ORIENTAL AND EUROPEAN NOODLES Oriental noodles are manufactured from a variety of wheat flours, vegetable starches, and rice flours. Wheat flour noodles (non-egg and egg noodles) are sold fresh and frozen in plastic bags (chow mein is the most familiar); vegetable starch noodles (mung bean or cellophane noodles) are usually sold dried in cellophane packages; and rice flour noodles (rice stick or rice vermicelli and fresh rice noodles) are sold both fresh and dried. Buckwheat noodles (soba) are sold dried in clear plastic packages. These noodles are available in Oriental food stores and some health food stores.

FRESH PASTA Freshly made or home-made pasta is softer and more delicately flavored than dried. Because of its moisture content, fresh pasta cooks in a matter of seconds or minutes depending on the thickness of the pasta type or whether it has been allowed to dry. Also, when portioning, remember that fresh pasta weighs more than dried and therefore 1½ more ounces will be needed per ¾ pound serving and 2 ounces more for a 1 pound serving.

Fresh noodles can be prepared in several ways: with all-purpose flour, eggs, salt, and no water; with only all-purpose flour, water, and salt; or with a mixture of finely milled durum wheat, all-purpose flour, and water. All can be made by hand mixing and rolling, or with a food processor, or manual pasta machine. If you wish to make your own pasta, there are excellent recipes in *The Classic Italian Cookbook*, by Marcella Hazan, and *The Fine Art of Italian Cooking*, by Giuliano Bugialli.

Ingredients are sometimes added to make beautifully colored pastas. Tomatoes or carrots for orange, spinach for green, beets for red, cocoa for brown, even squid's ink for black. Herbs, too, can be added to the dough for a lovely flecked pasta. The flavor is not changed much by these additions – just the look.

Fresh pasta can be bought at specialty shops and some supermarkets.

QUANTITIES It is very difficult to give the exact number of servings for pasta because there are so many variables. In Italy, 3½ to 4 ounces per serving is the rule of thumb, though the Italians don't typically eat pasta as a main course as we often do in North America. I find that 3 ounces is about right for each main dish serving of the long, thin pastas such as spaghetti, depending on how substantial or rich the sauce is. For side dishes and first courses, I use the same amount because I find that people gobble it up whether it is served as a side dish or a main dish. For tubular pastas such as penne or rigatoni, I generally measure ½ pound for 2 to 4 servings and ¾ pound for 4 to 6. Again, it depends on the richness or quantity of the sauce. Adjust quantities to suit the appetites of your family and friends.

I use a kitchen scale to weigh my pasta, but it is easy to divide each 1-pound package into quarters and go from there.

HOW TO COOK

Pasta is one of the simplest foods to cook, yet one of the easiest to ruin by overcooking.

For up to 1 pound of pasta, bring 4 to 6 quarts of water to a furious boil. The strands will stick together if not cooked in enough liquid. Just before adding the pasta, stir in 1½ to 2 tablespoons salt, if desired. Do not add oil. Add pasta to the boiling water all at once (spaghetti or other long pastas should be pushed down with a wooden spoon until completely submerged – never broken into smaller pieces) and immediately begin stirring with a wooden spoon. Cover the pot briefly to bring quickly back to a boil, then remove cover or the water will boil over. Stir again to separate pieces and place the lid halfway on to maintain a rapid boil. Remove lid occasionally and stir until pasta is *al dente*, which means the pasta is completely tender but still firm and chewy. Be careful, too, not to undercook it or it will be completely inedible.

Just-made noodles take only seconds to cook, store-bought fresh noodles will take 1 to 2 minutes, while dried pasta can take up to 15 minutes. After a few minutes, when the dried pasta is limp, begin testing for doneness by biting into a piece. Do not rely on the package instructions which are invariably several minutes too long. Continue biting a piece every few minutes until the white core has almost disappeared and the texture is done to your taste.

The moment the pasta is done, immediately drain in a colander (do not rinse unless the recipe specifies or the sauce will not cling), then shake it to remove excess water – especially important with the tubular and shell-shaped pastas. The instant the pasta is drained, it must be tossed with the sauce you have prepared. If not, it will continue cooking and stick together. Some cooks toss the drained pasta with a little olive oil or butter to separate the strands, but this is unnecessary unless the recipe specifies it.

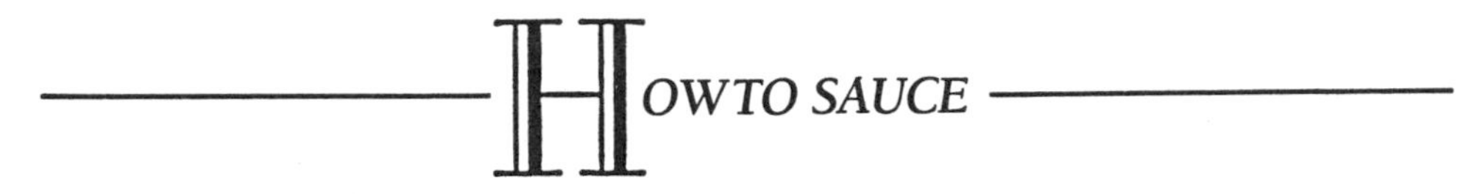

HOW TO SAUCE

Unlimited in scope, there are sauces for every taste and every shape of pasta and then some. I've heard it said that, in Italy, you could eat a different sauce daily for a year and never have the same one twice.

Sauces can range from the quick and simple butter and cheese to the more complex, long-cooked ragus. Feel free to mix and match sauces to pasta, just keeping in mind that there are a few basic, yet breakable rules (you needn't be as strict as the Italians!) for matching sauce to pasta.

The different shapes, sizes, and surfaces all function in a special way to gather up the different sauces and ingredients. In general, long thin noodles such as spaghetti, linguine, and capellini go well with uncooked or light sauces based on tomatoes, vegetables, seafood, or olive oil (pesto, garlic and oil, and clam sauce, for example). Long flat shapes such as fresh fettuccine match perfectly with delicate cream or cheese sauces. Thicker, tubular shapes – penne and rigatoni – pair well with meat and vegetable sauces. Shells – conchiglie and lumache – and cup-shapes like orecchiette prefer small bits of vegetables, meats, and fish in a plentiful sauce that can be caught up in the hollows. Fusilli or rotelle – any of the twisted or wheel varieties – need sauces that are not too thick or chunky so that they can wrap themselves around the smallish bits. Pappardelle, a wide, fresh ribbon pasta, is famous for being paired with rabbit sauce, but can be matched with other assertive meat sauces.

Though you can match any sauce to whatever type of pasta you wish, it is best to substitute one as similar in shape and texture as the one recommended in the recipe. When saucing pasta, the general rule is to pair light sauces with the delicate, long pastas and robust sauces with the heavier pasta shapes. But the biggest crime against pasta is oversaucing. A little sauce left at the bottom of the serving dish is fine, but pasta should never be swimming or drowning in a sauce.

While testing recipes for this book I was surprised to discover that cream and tomato sauces do not need to be cooked down until heavily thickened: with few exceptions, these sauces need only to thicken slightly. They will taste much lighter and truer cooked this way.

I have given cooking times in my recipes, but there are so many variables that it is hard to give exact cooking times. In the end, the sauce should cling nicely to the pasta. It should be neither too thick and heavy – guaranteed to turn pasta into a goopy mess – nor should the sauce fail to cling to the pasta because of undercooking. At worst, if the sauce doesn't cling thoroughly you can put the pasta – sauce and all – back into the skillet and stir over low heat until thickened properly. But please be careful not to overcook it or you will ruin the pasta itself.

There is an Italian saying: "Guests must wait for the pasta, pasta never waits for the guests," which means the sauce should be ready to use the instant the pasta is drained. I always prepare my sauce while the pasta is boiling or cook it first and have it ready in the skillet or saucepan with the element turned off. When the pasta is at the *al dente* stage, I turn the heat back on to gently reheat the sauce while I am draining the pasta. I immediately toss the two together and serve at once.

The same rules of matching pasta shapes to sauces do not apply to Oriental noodles because there is only one shape – long. In Asian cuisines, noodles are matched instead with cooking techniques, such as fried fresh noodles (chow mein), deep-fried or braised bean thread noodles, or hot or cold sauced buckwheat noodles.

HOW TO SERVE

Once the pasta is drained, put it immediately into a wide, shallow serving bowl about 12 inches in diameter and 2½ inches deep. Special pasta serving bowls can be purchased in most gourmet shops. Next, pour the sauce over the pasta and immediately begin tossing gently with two forks. (Some cooks prefer to add the drained pasta to the sauce in the skillet and toss it there before placing in a serving bowl or dividing it onto individual heated plates.) Connoisseurs of pasta never use metal tools for tossing or serving their pasta; instead they use specially designed wooden spoons or forks with spikes. These, too, can be found in most gourmet shops, but I find that metal dinner forks do just as well. I also place a large serving spoon in the bowl to help take up the sauce ingredients at the bottom of the dish.

To remove long, thin strands to a plate, lift a small portion of pasta well up over the serving dish and then place it on heated plates or wide bowls. Wide, slightly shallow bowls are traditionally used for individual pasta servings because they help keep the pasta warm longer and hold the sauce and pasta together. I prefer bowls for rustic pasta dishes and plates for more elegant ones. When dishing up, don't forget to scoop out the ingredients that are always hiding at the bottom of the serving dish, then divide them evenly among individual heated bowls or plates.

HOW TO EAT

A lot of people wonder about the correct way to eat pasta, especially the long thin forms. The answer is, untimidly and with great gusto – and without a lot of consideration given to eating too tidily!

Both the Italians and the Orientals think it is just fine to noisily slurp their noodles, and I heartily agree with them. The Chinese and Japanese use chopsticks to transfer strands of noodles to the mouth and then they literally suck them in. The Italians pick up a few long strands with a fork and twirl them around a couple of times until a bundle forms with a few strands still dangling. (If the pasta is correctly cooked this will happen; if overcooked the strands will wrap all too neatly around the fork.) Sometimes they place the tip of their fork against their bowl or plate to assist in the twirling. Some non-Italians find it necessary to use a large spoon as a base to twirl their pasta. This is not correct and most Italians think it gauche. While Italian restaurants often provide customers with a spoon, this is meant either to help toss the pasta or to scoop up some kinds of sauces.

INGREDIENTS

ANCHOVIES: My recipes use the canned anchovy fillets in oil.

BLACK OLIVES: I use Kalamata olives from Greece. You may also use Niçoise olives from France. They are available in supermarket delis or specialty food shops. Canned American olives do not have the flavor or pungency needed for these recipes.

BLACK PEPPER: I always use freshly ground black peppercorns. When I suggest "lots of freshly ground black pepper," I mean at least 20 grindings of the pepper mill. In addition, most sauces need a few extra grindings of pepper at the table.

CAPERS: These are the unopened flower buds of a Mediterranean shrub. Many cooks prefer the tiny French capers but I use the large variety in my pasta sauces because they have a stronger flavor. They are packed in vinegar (not salt), and I never rinse them.

CHILI PASTE WITH SOY BEAN: This hot and spicy condiment is widely used in China and adds a fiery taste and red tint to sauces. It is available in Oriental food stores.

CORIANDER: A pungent herb also known as cilantro or Chinese parsley.

DRIED HERBS: The fresher the dried herbs, the more flavorful your cooking. To release their flavor, crumble them in your fingers before adding them to the sauce. If they have lost their color and aroma it is best to replace them.

FRESH HERBS: Do not substitute dried herbs if fresh are called for in a recipe.

GARLIC: It is hard to imagine anyone not cooking with garlic (lots of it!), for it is a seasoning that goes with almost every savory dish. Choose large bulbs that are tightly closed and not sprouting. Squeeze the bulb to make sure it is firm and fresh. Avoid powdered garlic.

GORGONZOLA: A very creamy, mold-ripened cheese from the Lombardy region of Italy. Its sharp flavor is wonderful in cream sauces. It is available in Italian food shops or well-stocked cheese stores.

OLIVE OIL: I prefer using an extra-virgin (first-pressing) oil with a delicate olive taste.

PANCETTA: An Italian-style bacon that is unsmoked, seasoned with pepper and spices, then rolled. It is found mainly at Italian food markets.

PARMESAN: Be sure to purchase Parmesan that has the words "Parmigiano Reggiano" or, second best, "Grana Padano" stamped on the rind. Always grate it fresh just before using because it begins to lose flavor after grating. It is available in Italian food shops or well-stocked cheese stores.

PINE NUTS (PIGNOLI): These small, mild, sweetly flavored nuts do not have any substitutes. They go rancid quite quickly, so I usually refrigerate or freeze them. They are available in most specialty food shops and some supermarkets.

PROSCIUTTO: This salted, air-dried Italian ham is available in Italian food shops and at some supermarket deli counters.

RICOTTA: Fresh ricotta resembles cottage cheese in that it is a soft, white curd cheese, but it is finer in taste and texture. They are not interchangeable. It is available in Italian food shops and some supermarkets.

SAMBAL OELEK: This bottled preparation of crushed red peppers and salt is used in Indonesian cooking. It is available in Oriental food shops.

SHALLOTS: These have a delicate onion-garlic flavor. If unavailable, I often substitute a little minced garlic and onion.

SQUID: To clean, gently pull head and body apart. Cut off the tentacles just in front of the eyes. Squeeze out the beak, located where the tentacles come together (it looks like a small white marble) and discard. Under cold running water, remove all the entrails inside the body sac. Peel off the purple membrane covering the body. Set aside tentacles and cleaned body sac and continue until all are cleaned. Rinse tentacles and follow recipe instructions.

SUN-DRIED TOMATOES: These have become very popular in North America in the past few years. Pumate San Remo from Liguria, Italy, is considered the best brand. They are available in most specialty and Italian food shops.

TOMATOES, CANNED: The best canned tomatoes come from the San Marzano region in Italy, but they are difficult to find. Buy the best Italian or domestic brands available (experiment until you find a brand you like), for it makes an enormous difference in the taste and quality of sauces. Crush them in your hands as you add them to your sauce or crush them in the skillet with a wooden spoon if you don't like getting your hands messy.

TOMATOES, FRESH: Use only flavorful, ripe, unwaxed tomatoes. If not fully ripe when you purchase them, do not refrigerate; instead, allow them to ripen at room temperature. There is no need to skin or seed tomatoes unless specified.

TORTA DI GORGONZOLA: This cheese is made by layering Gorgonzola and mascarpone cheese. Mascarpone is similar to cream cheese, but sweeter and creamier and more delicately flavored. It is available in Italian food shops or well-stocked cheese stores.

VERMOUTH: I use dry white vermouth in my recipes instead of dry white wine. You may substitute dry white wine, of course.

WILD MUSHROOMS: Many exotic fungi are now available at specialty food shops. *Oyster Mushrooms* are cultivated and also grow wild. The flesh is firm and white or gray in color. *Shiitake Mushrooms* are an umbrella-shaped brownish black variety that were once only available dried. *Cèpes/Porcini* have a sweet, nutty flavor and are available mostly in the fall. *Chanterelles*, egg-yolk colored and funnel-shaped, have a delicate but distinct flavor with a slight apricot aroma. *Morels* are considered by many to be the peerless mushroom. They are pitted like a honeycomb and have a tendency to trap sand. Wash them carefully but do not allow them to soak.

ZEST: The colored outer layer of skin on a citrus fruit.

EQUIPMENT

COLANDER: It should have legs or a stand to hold it upright in the sink. The larger it is, the better.

CHEESE GRATER: For grating Parmesan or other hard cheeses. I also use the four-sided cheese grater for finely grated zest (the smallest openings) and for grated zest (the largest openings).

FOOD PROCESSOR: Excellent for grating hard cheeses and for puréeing sauces.

HEAVY SKILLETS AND SAUCEPANS: Flimsy skillets and saucepans are not recommended. You should also have noncorrosive pans for making sauces with lemon juice or tomatoes.

LARGE POT: You will need a pot that holds at least six quarts for cooking pasta.

PASTA SERVING BOWL: These wide, shallow bowls about 12 inches in diameter and 2½ inches deep help retain the heat longer than a serving platter.

PEPPER MILL: Essential for cooking and for the table.

RUBBER SPATULA: A spatula is handy for scraping out the sauce ingredients from the skillet onto the pasta.

SPAGHETTI COOKER: These large pots have a built-in strainer and although I have never used one, I know a lot of people who swear by them.

SPAGHETTI SPOON OR FORK: These plastic or wooden pronged utensils are for lifting strands of spaghetti from the cooking pot or for tossing pasta with sauce. Most Italians prefer them but I find dinner forks work just as well.

WOODEN SPOONS: Better than metal spoons for stirring pasta or sauces.

SAUCES

Redolent with garlic, this rustic, classic Italian sauce can be made in a flash. ♦ Feel free to add more(!) or use less garlic to your own taste, but be careful not to allow it to brown or burn, or the sauce will be bitter.

Garlic and Oil Sauce

¼ cup best-quality olive oil
15 large garlic cloves, chopped
¼ teaspoon hot red pepper flakes, or to taste
½ cup finely chopped fresh parsley
Salt
Lots of freshly ground black pepper
¼ cup freshly grated Parmesan cheese

HEAT OIL in a medium skillet. Add garlic, red pepper flakes, and parsley and cook until garlic is tender, about 4 minutes. Stir in salt and pepper and toss with hot pasta in a serving bowl. Sprinkle Parmesan cheese over pasta and toss again.

Pass extra grated cheese and the pepper mill for each person to add to taste. Serves 4.

Recommended Pasta: ¾ pound spaghetti or spaghettini

When you feel like splurging.

CAVIAR SAUCE

2 to 3 tablespoons butter
4 ounces (113-g jar) salmon caviar
Freshly ground black pepper
1 lemon, cut into thin wedges

PUT BUTTER in a serving bowl and add drained pasta. Toss until butter is completely melted and evenly distributed.

Divide pasta onto warm plates, and top each portion with a heaping spoonful of caviar. Add a liberal grinding of pepper, place a lemon wedge on each plate, and serve at once. Serves 2 to 4.

Recommended Pasta: ½ pound capellini

This classic Genoese sauce has countless variations. Some are made with pecans, walnuts, or almonds instead of pine nuts; some use all basil and no parsley; others use a combination of Parmesan and Romano cheese. ♦ Also, many cooks add a little butter or cream to lighten the mixture while tossing the sauce and pasta.

PESTO SAUCE

3 medium garlic cloves
1 cup fresh basil leaves, washed and patted dry
½ cup roughly chopped fresh parsley
¼ cup pine nuts, lightly toasted in a dry skillet*
½ cup best-quality olive oil
¾ cup freshly grated Parmesan cheese
Salt
Lots of freshly ground black pepper

COMBINE GARLIC, basil, parsley, and pine nuts in the bowl of a food processor. Continue processing and add oil in a slow, steady stream.

Stop the machine and add cheese, salt, and pepper. Turn on machine and process a few seconds to combine. Taste for seasoning, then toss with hot pasta. Serve promptly. Serves 4.

Recommended Pasta: ¾ pound capellini, spaghetti, or linguine

*NOTE: Spread pine nuts in a single layer in an unoiled, heavy skillet. Place on moderate heat and stir occasionally until lightly browned.

UNCOOKED SUN-DRIED TOMATO AND OLIVE SAUCE

- 10 large sun-dried tomatoes in olive oil, drained
- 2 tablespoons sun-dried tomato oil or best-quality olive oil
- 12 Greek olives (Kalamata), pitted and finely chopped
- 1 large green onion (green part only), finely chopped
- Lots of freshly ground black pepper
- ¼ cup freshly grated Parmesan cheese

PROCESS SUN-DRIED TOMATOES and oil in a food processor until the tomatoes become a rough paste.

Toss tomato mixture, olives, green onion, and pepper with hot pasta. Add Parmesan cheese and toss again.

Pass extra grated cheese and the pepper mill for each person to add to taste. Serves 2 to 3.

Recommended Pasta: ½ pound fusilli

ippy and intriguing — and all it takes is a quick whirl in a food processor!

If you enjoy pesto sauce, you will surely enjoy this recipe which uses similar ingredients. Pesto sauce was traditionally made in a mortar and pestle; today, it's usually prepared in a food processor. ♦ Here the ingredients are not puréed, but simply mixed, then combined with the hot pasta.

Uncooked Basil, Pine Nut, and Parmesan Sauce

¼ cup best-quality olive oil
3 large garlic cloves, minced
½ cup pine nuts, lightly toasted in a dry skillet*
¼ teaspoon salt
Lots of freshly ground black pepper
2 cups shredded fresh basil leaves, plus 2 whole leaves for garnish
⅓ cup freshly grated Parmesan cheese

In a small bowl, mix oil, garlic, pine nuts, salt, and pepper. In another bowl, lightly toss basil and Parmesan cheese.

Drain pasta and immediately place it in a serving bowl. Add oil-garlic mixture and toss until evenly distributed. Add basil-cheese mixture and toss gently until mixed. Garnish with basil and serve.

Pass extra grated cheese and the pepper mill for each person to add to taste. Serves 4.

Recommended Pasta: ¾ pound linguine or spaghettini

*Note: Spread pine nuts in a single layer in an unoiled, heavy skillet. Place on moderate heat and stir occasionally until lightly browned.

Orange, Olive, and Basil Sauce

¼ cup (2 ounces/½ stick) butter
Finely grated zest of 2 large oranges
20 Greek olives (Kalamata), pitted and chopped
2 large garlic cloves, finely chopped
Juice from 1 large orange (about ⅓ cup)
Lots of freshly ground black pepper
⅓ cup chopped fresh basil leaves
¼ cup freshly grated Parmesan cheese

MELT BUTTER in a medium skillet. Add orange zest, olives, and garlic, and cook for 1 minute. Add orange juice and pepper and cook for another minute. Toss with hot pasta, add basil and Parmesan cheese, and toss again. Serve at once.

Pass extra grated cheese and the pepper mill for each person to add to taste. Serves 4.

Recommended Pasta: ¾ pound spaghetti or linguine

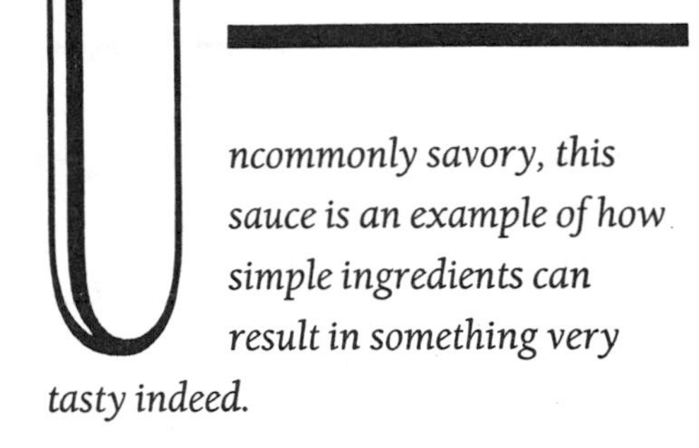

ncommonly savory, this sauce is an example of how simple ingredients can result in something very tasty indeed.

A lively, unusual, Asian inspired sauce flavored with pungent chili paste, balsamic vinegar, and coriander leaves.

Almond Butter Soy Sauce

½ cup (4 ounces/1 stick) butter
½ cup unblanched almonds, coarsely chopped in a food processor
1 small garlic clove, minced
½ teaspoon powdered ginger
½ teaspoon sugar
1 teaspoon soy sauce
1 teaspoon chili paste with soy bean
1 teaspoon Oriental sesame oil
1 teaspoon balsamic vinegar
¼ cup chopped fresh coriander leaves

CUT BUTTER into pieces and place in a serving bowl. Add remaining ingredients (no need to stir) except coriander. Toss with hot pasta until butter is melted, add coriander, and toss again. Serves 4.

Recommended Pasta: ¾ pound spaghetti or Chinese egg noodles

Invite only your most au courant friends over to enjoy this gutsy sauce. It is not for the fainthearted – just for those who love the rustic, sensual flavors of the Mediterranean.

Green Olive Sauce

1 large garlic clove
12-ounce (375-mL) jar pimiento-stuffed green olives, drained
⅓ cup roughly chopped fresh parsley
¼ cup best-quality olive oil
2 tablespoons fresh lemon juice
Lots of freshly ground black pepper

IN A FOOD PROCESSOR mince garlic. Add olives and parsley and chop – do not over-process into a paste. Add remaining ingredients and process a few seconds to combine. Toss with hot pasta in a serving bowl and serve right away.

No cheese with this sauce, please. Serves 4.

Recommended Pasta: ¾ pound linguine or spaghetti

What could be simpler than tossing pasta with some butter and cheese? ♦ It is quick, delicious, and eminently satisfying — and with a green salad it makes a complete meal.

BUTTER AND CHEESE SAUCE

- ½ cup (4 ounces/1 stick) butter, at room temperature
- ½ cup freshly grated Parmesan cheese
- Salt
- Lots of freshly ground black pepper

CUT BUTTER into pieces and place in a serving bowl. Add drained pasta and toss with butter until completely melted. Add Parmesan cheese, salt, and pepper, and toss again. Serve at once. Serves 4.

Recommended Pasta: ¾ pound spaghetti, capellini, or linguine

Butter Ginger Sauce

- ½ cup (4 ounces/1 stick) butter
- 3 tablespoons grated fresh ginger
- 4 large garlic cloves, finely chopped
- ½ teaspoon hot red pepper flakes, or to taste
- 1 teaspoon dried basil
- 4 whole green onions, finely chopped
- Lot of freshly ground black pepper
- ¼ cup freshly grated Parmesan cheese

MELT BUTTER in a medium skillet. Add everything except cheese and cook until garlic is tender, about 4 minutes. Combine with hot pasta, toss with cheese, and serve. Serves 4.

Recommended Pasta: ¾ pound capellini, spaghettini, or linguine

Quite refreshing, fragrant, and unusual. This pasta sauce has Oriental overtones and makes a delightful first course dish. ♦ *Grate the ginger on the small, round openings of a cheese grater.*

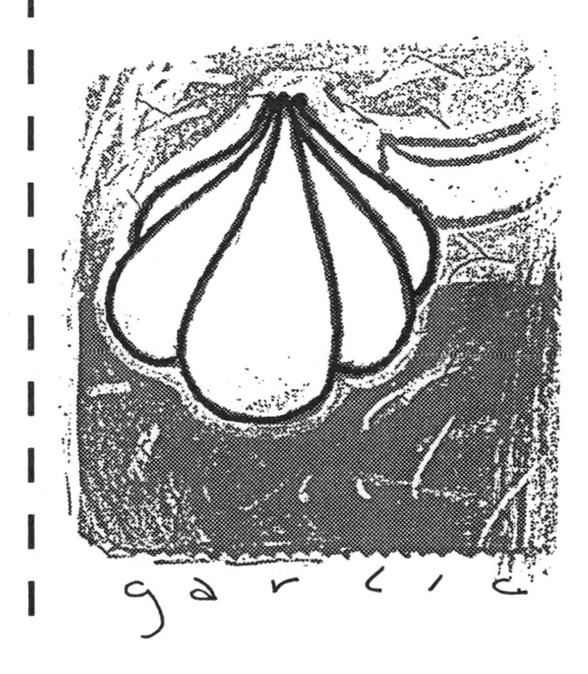

I think of this as the elegant cousin of Garlic and Oil Sauce. The butter gives this sauce a mellower and more refined flavor. ♦ It is surprisingly tasty for such a simple sauce.

BUTTER GARLIC SAUCE

¼ cup (2 ounces/½ stick) butter
10 large garlic cloves, thinly sliced (not chopped or minced)
Salt
Lots of freshly ground black pepper
Grated Parmesan cheese

MELT BUTTER in a small skillet. Add garlic and cook until tender, about 4 minutes. Do not brown. Toss with hot pasta in a serving bowl, sprinkle with salt and pepper, then toss again.

Pass grated Parmesan cheese and the pepper mill for each person to add to taste. Serves 2 to 4.

Recommended Pasta: 10 ounces spaghettini or linguine

CHEESE & EGG

SAUCES

♦ ♦ ♦

Elegant, easy, and simply divine. This sauce was created by a Roman chef named Alfredo. ♦ For best results, serve it over fresh fettuccine.

ALFREDO SAUCE

½ cup (4 ounces/1 stick) butter
¼ cup heavy or whipping cream
1 cup freshly grated Parmesan cheese
⅛ teaspoon freshly grated nutmeg
Salt
Lots of freshly ground black pepper

PUT BUTTER and cream in a shallow, ovenproof serving bowl and place in a 200° oven while boiling pasta.

Drain pasta, remove serving bowl from oven, and toss pasta with butter-cream mixture until well distributed. Add Parmesan cheese, nutmeg, salt, and pepper. Toss again and serve. Serves 4.

Recommended Pasta: ¾ pound fresh fettuccine

Carbonara Sauce

2 large eggs
1/3 cup heavy cream
1/4 teaspoon freshly grated nutmeg
1/4 teaspoon salt
Lots of freshly ground black pepper
3/4 pound bacon, cut into 1/2-inch pieces
2 large garlic cloves, minced
1 large ripe tomato, choppped
1/4 cup freshly grated Parmesan cheese

IN A LARGE, wide serving bowl, whisk eggs, cream, nutmeg, salt, and pepper until blended. Set aside.

In a small skillet, cook bacon until crisp. Transfer to a paper towel-lined plate to drain, reserving 1 teaspoon bacon fat.

In same skillet with reserved bacon fat, cook garlic over medium heat for 1 minute. Add tomato; cook for 5 minutes or until soft. Set aside.

Drain cooked pasta and immediately place on top of egg mixture. Toss gently until pasta is coated with sauce. Add cooked tomato; toss. Garnish with cooked bacon and Parmesan cheese.

Pass extra grated cheese and the pepper mill for each person to add to taste. Serves 4 to 6.

Recommended Pasta: 3/4 pound spaghetti or linguine

This updated classic is deliciously satisfying. ♦ *I've added tomatoes and substituted crisp bacon for the traditional prosciutto or pancetta.*

A luscious and creamy sauce. Pure heaven.

Mascarpone-Gorgonzola Sauce

- 2 tablespoons butter
- 1 cup heavy or whipping cream
- ¾ pound mascarpone with Gorgonzola cheese (Torta di Gorgonzola)
- ½ cup freshly grated Parmesan cheese
- Salt
- Lots of freshly ground black pepper

MELT BUTTER in a medium, heavy skillet. Add cream and cook at a gentle boil until sauce thickens slightly. Stir in cheeses, salt, and pepper, and continue cooking until reduced slightly. Do not let the mixture boil. Serve immediately over hot pasta. Serves 4 to 6.

Recommended Pasta: 1 pound capellini, linguine, or spaghetti

Gorgonzola Sauce

- 1 cup heavy or whipping cream
- ½ pound Gorgonzola cheese
- 2 tablespoons butter
- ¼ teaspoon freshly grated nutmeg
- Salt
- Lots of freshly ground black pepper
- ⅓ cup freshly grated Parmesan cheese

In a medium, heavy saucepan, cook cream at a gentle boil until it thickens slightly.

Lower heat and crumble in cheese (do not allow sauce to boil or cheese will separate). Add butter, nutmeg, salt, and pepper, and continue cooking until cheese is completely blended in. Stir in Parmesan cheese, taste for seasoning, and combine with hot pasta.

Pass extra grated Parmesan cheese and the pepper mill for each person to add to taste. Serves 4 to 6.

Recommended Pasta: 1 pound capellini, linguine, spaghetti, or fettuccine

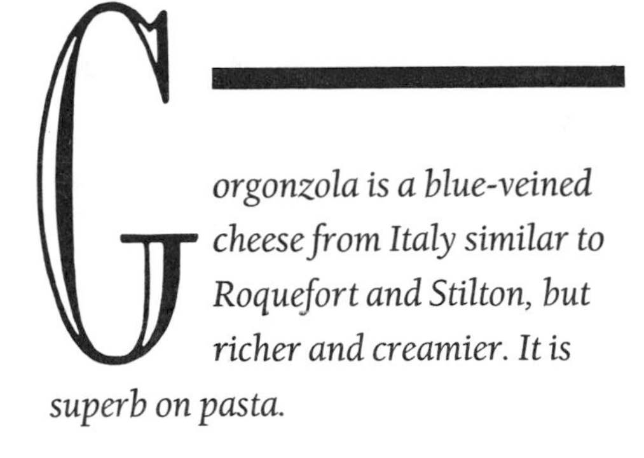

Gorgonzola is a blue-veined cheese from Italy similar to Roquefort and Stilton, but richer and creamier. It is superb on pasta.

When you need solace in a hurry, whip up this comforting sauce. It is reminiscent of macaroni and cheese, but quicker because it doesn't need baking.

CHEDDAR SCALLION SAUCE

½ cup heavy or whipping cream
1 tablespoon Dijon-style mustard
Salt
Lots of freshly ground black pepper
½ pound Cheddar cheese, grated
4 whole green onions (scallions), finely chopped

IN A WIDE, shallow serving bowl, beat cream and mustard with a fork until combined. Add salt and pepper; stir.

Drain pasta and immediately place on top of cream mixture. Toss gently until pasta is coated and continue tossing, at the same time adding cheese and green onions in three additions. Serve at once.

Pass the pepper mill for each person to add to taste. Serves 4.

Recommended Pasta: ¾ pound spaghetti

Hot, Hot Ricotta Sauce

½ cup (4 ounces/1 stick) butter
1 cup ricotta cheese
½ cup freshly grated Parmesan cheese
2 tablespoons chopped fresh basil leaves, plus ⅓ cup for garnish
¼ cup heavy or whipping cream
Lots of freshly ground black pepper
2¼ teaspoons cayenne, or to taste

MELT BUTTER in a large skillet. Stir in remaining ingredients. Cook for about 5 minutes and toss with hot pasta in a serving bowl. Garnish with basil and toss again at the table.

Pass extra grated Parmesan cheese for each person to sprinkle to taste. Serves 6.

Recommended Pasta: 1 pound linguine or spaghetti

For a truly unusual hot sauce, the ricotta is tinted pink with cayenne. The sauce looks a lot more appetizing once it is tossed with the pasta than it does in the skillet!

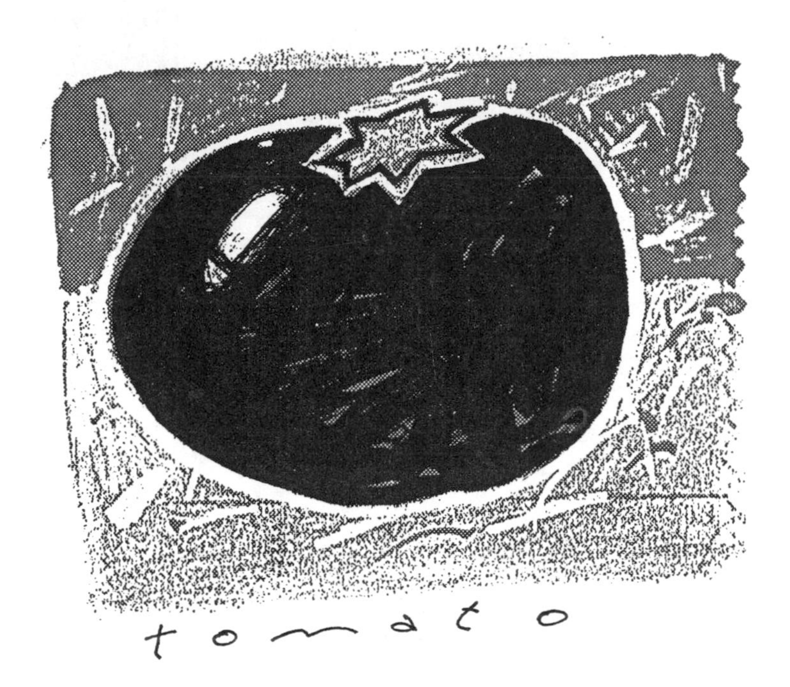
tomato

SAUCES

♦ ♦ ♦

Make this sauce if you are partial to sun-dried tomatoes. Its pretty appearance and lovely flavor belie its easy preparation.

Creamy Sun-Dried Tomato Sauce

2 tablespoons butter
2 large garlic cloves, finely chopped
20 large sun-dried tomatoes in olive oil, drained and sliced lengthwise into ¼-inch pieces
1 cup heavy or whipping cream
⅔ cup chopped fresh basil leaves, plus 3 tablespoons for garnish
Salt
Lots of freshly ground black pepper
Grated Parmesan cheese

MELT BUTTER in a heavy saucepan. Add garlic and cook for 1 minute. Add sun-dried tomatoes and cream and cook at a gentle boil until sauce thickens slightly. Stir in basil, salt, and pepper, and cook for another minute. Taste for seasoning and toss with hot pasta in a serving bowl. Garnish with chopped basil and serve immediately.

Pass grated Parmesan cheese and the pepper mill for each person to add to taste. Serves 2 to 4.

Recommended Pasta: ¾ pound linguine or spaghetti

Fresh Tomato and Basil Sauce

½ cup (4 ounces/1 stick) butter
2 large garlic cloves, minced
3 medium ripe tomatoes, (1 pound), seeded and cut into 1-inch cubes
¼ cup dry white vermouth
¼ cup chicken broth
Lots of freshly ground black pepper
Salt
⅔ cup roughly chopped fresh basil leaves, plus 3 tablespoons for garnish
Grated Parmesan cheese

MELT BUTTER in a medium, noncorrosive skillet. Add garlic and tomatoes and cook for 5 minutes, or until tomatoes are softened. Add vermouth and cook on high heat until slightly thickened, about 4 minutes. Add broth and continue to cook on high heat for 2 minutes longer, or until sauce thickens slightly.

Stir in pepper, salt, and basil. Taste for seasoning, toss with hot pasta in a serving bowl, and garnish with basil.

Pass grated Parmesan cheese for each person to sprinkle to taste. Serves 4.

Recommended Pasta: ¾ pound capellini or linguine

Elegant and simple, this wonderfully fresh-tasting tomato sauce, infused with the heady perfume of fresh basil, is perfect for entertaining. ♦ *Do not use canned tomatoes or dried basil for this dish.*

My favorite accompaniment to bacon and eggs is thickly sliced ripe tomatoes sautéed in butter with lots of freshly cracked (very coarsely ground) pepper. I always thought the combination would be heavenly on pasta, so I experimented with the ingredients and came up with this. ♦ It is quite hot, so if you want to cool it down a bit, just use less Tabasco and black pepper.

Hot and Peppery Tomato Sauce

¼ cup (2 ounces/½ stick) butter
3 large ripe tomatoes (1¼ pounds), chopped
1½ teaspoons freshly cracked black pepper
1 teaspoon Tabasco, or to taste
¼ cup freshly grated Parmesan cheese

MELT BUTTER in a small, heavy, noncorrosive skillet. Add tomatoes, pepper, and Tabasco. Turn heat to high and cook until slightly thickened, about 10 minutes.

Toss with hot pasta in a serving bowl, then add Parmesan cheese and toss again. Allow the pasta to sit a few minutes to absorb some of the sauce's flavor. The sauce will thicken a bit more on standing.

Pass extra grated cheese for each person to sprinkle to taste. Serves 2 to 4.

Recommended Pasta: 10 ounces spaghettini or linguine

ANOTHER FRESH TOMATO SAUCE

- ¼ cup best-quality olive oil
- 6 large garlic cloves, chopped
- 1 large shallot, finely chopped
- 6 medium ripe tomatoes (2 pounds) seeded and cut into 1-inch cubes
- 1 teaspoon sugar
- 1 teaspoon dried basil
- 2 teaspoons Tabasco, or to taste
- Salt
- Lots of freshly ground black pepper
- ¼ cup freshly grated Parmesan cheese

HEAT OIL in a large, heavy, noncorrosive skillet. Add garlic and shallot and cook for 2 minutes. Add tomatoes, sugar, basil, Tabasco, salt, and pepper, and cook for 15 minutes, or until tomatoes are thickened. Taste for seasoning and toss with hot pasta in a serving bowl. Add Parmesan cheese and toss again.

Pass extra grated cheese for each person to sprinkle to taste. Serves 4.

Recommended Pasta: ¾ pound capellini, spaghetti, or linguine

What a revelation this sauce will be to those who have tasted only thick tomato sauces made with canned tomatoes and tomato paste. ◆ *Don't leave out the Tabasco altogether; it adds that little extra zip.*

Mexican salsa was the inspiration for this sauce. It is almost identical to Uncooked Tomato Sauce with Olives, Capers, and Mozzarella but it tastes entirely different because of the different seasonings. ♦ Coriander fans will adore it.

Uncooked Tomato Sauce with Coriander

3 medium ripe tomatoes (1 pound), seeded and cut into 1-inch cubes
⅓ cup best-quality olive oil
3 large garlic cloves, minced
3 to 4 teaspoons sambal oelek or 1 to 2 tablespoons seeded, finely chopped fresh jalapeño peppers
6 ounces Monterey Jack or mozzarella cheese, cut into ½-inch cubes
½ cup roughly chopped fresh coriander leaves
¼ cup freshly grated Parmesan cheese
½ teaspoon freshly ground black pepper
Salt
Grated Parmesan cheese

Combine sauce ingredients in a medium, noncorrosive bowl and set aside for 30 minutes – no longer.

Cook pasta until al dente, drain in a colander, and immediately return the empty pot to the turned-off burner. Pour in sauce, add drained pasta, and toss to coat evenly. Cover pot for 1 minute to gently heat the pasta and partially melt the cheese. Uncover, then place in a large serving bowl, and serve immediately.

Freshly grated Parmesan cheese may be served as an accompaniment if desired. Serves 4.

Recommended Pasta: ¾ pound linguine or spaghetti

Uncooked Tomato Sauce with Olives, Capers, and Mozzarella

3 medium ripe tomatoes (1 pound), seeded and cut into 1-inch cubes
1/3 cup best-quality olive oil
3 large garlic cloves, minced
10 Greek olives (Kalamata), pitted and chopped
2 tablespoons capers, drained
6 ounces mozzarella cheese, cut into 1/2-inch cubes
1 1/2 teaspoons dried oregano
1/4 cup freshly grated Parmesan cheese
1/2 teaspoon freshly ground black pepper
Salt

COMBINE SAUCE ingredients in a medium, noncorrosive bowl, and set aside for 30 minutes or up to 2 hours — no longer.

Cook pasta until al dente, drain in a colander, and immediately return the empty pot to the turned-off burner. Pour in sauce, add drained pasta, and toss to coat evenly. Cover pot for 1 minute to gently heat the pasta and partially melt the cheese. Uncover, then place in a serving bowl and serve immediately.

Pass extra grated cheese and the pepper mill for each person to sprinkle to taste. Serves 4.

Recommended Pasta: 3/4 pound linguine or spaghetti.

This colorful, zesty, fast, and easy sauce is one of my all-time favorites. The ingredients are simply tossed in a bowl and allowed to sit a while until the flavors meld. ♦ *If you make it with anything less than ripe, flavorful, and unwaxed tomatoes you will be disappointed — the quality of this sauce is directly proportionate to the quality of the tomatoes.*

Toasted pecans, garlic, and tomatoes are an unexpected and interesting combination of textures and flavors. ♦ Be careful not to burn the pecans or the sauce will be bitter.

Pecan Tomato Sauce

½ cup (4 ounces/1 stick) butter
1 tablespoon best-quality olive oil
4 large garlic cloves, chopped
⅔ cup chopped pecans
3 medium ripe tomatoes (1 pound), cut into 1-inch cubes
Salt
Lots of freshly ground black pepper

MELT BUTTER with the oil in a large, noncorrosive skillet. Add garlic and pecans and cook until pecans are lightly toasted but not brown, about 2 minutes. Add tomatoes, salt, and pepper, and cook until slightly thickened, about 4 minutes. Toss with hot pasta in a serving bowl.

Serve with or without grated Parmesan cheese. Serves 4.

Recommended Pasta: ¾ pound spaghettini

PUTTANESCA SAUCE

- 3 tablespoons best-quality olive oil
- 6 large garlic cloves, chopped
- 28-ounce (796-mL) can tomatoes, undrained
- 12 Greek olives (Kalamata), pitted and chopped
- 2 tablespoons capers, drained
- ½ teaspoon hot red pepper flakes
- ½ cup finely chopped fresh parsley, plus 2 tablespoons for garnish
- Grated Parmesan cheese

HEAT OIL in a medium, heavy, noncorrosive skillet. Add garlic and cook for 2 minutes. Add tomatoes and liquid and cook for 30 minutes, or until sauce thickens slightly.

Just before pasta is ready, add remaining ingredients, then toss with hot pasta in a serving bowl. Garnish with parsley and serve immediately.

Pass extra grated cheese and the pepper mill for each person to add to taste. Serves 4.

Recommended Pasta: ½ pound penne or rigatoni

Legend has it that this lusty sauce was created by Neapolitan ladies of the night. Translated, puttanesca means "of a harlot or whore." ♦ *There are two stories: the ladies either cooked this quick and tasty sauce between clients or they prepared it to entice passersby with the tantalizing aroma!*

BLACK OLIVES

Here is a delicious, robust, and spicy version of Italian meat and tomato (Bolognese) sauce. ◆ *The success of this sauce rests on the use of excellent quality Italian sausage, though you can substitute ground pork for the sausage in a pinch. The amount of seasonings – hot pepper flakes, fennel seeds, and black pepper – will have to be increased to taste if using ground pork.*

TOMATO SAUCE WITH HOT ITALIAN SAUSAGE

- 1/4 cup (2 ounces / 1/2 stick) butter
- 2 medium onions, chopped
- 3 large garlic cloves, finely chopped
- 1 1/2 pounds hot Italian sausage, removed from casing
- 5 1/2-ounce can tomato paste
- 3-pound (48-ounce) can Italian plum tomatoes, undrained
- 3 tablespoons dried basil
- 1/4 teaspoon cinnamon
- 1 tablespoon fennel seeds
- 1/2 teaspoon hot red pepper flakes
- 1 1/2 teaspoons salt
- 1 teaspoon freshly ground black pepper
- Grated Parmesan cheese

MELT BUTTER in a large, heavy saucepan. Add onions and garlic and cook gently for 2 minutes. Add sausage and sauté, breaking up any lumps with a fork, until thoroughly cooked, about 5 minutes. Stir in tomato paste, tomatoes with liquid, and remaining ingredients except Parmesan cheese.

Simmer for 30 minutes, taste for seasoning – it should be hot and spicy – but do not overcook; it is not a thick tomato sauce.

Pass grated cheese for each person to sprinkle to taste.

Recommended Pasta: 1 1/2 pounds penne, rigatoni, linguine, spaghetti, or fusilli. Serves 8.

VEGETABLE, LEGUME & FRUIT

SAUCES

♦ ♦ ♦

Unusual, to say the least — but quite nice.

Apricot, Orange, and Basil Sauce

- ½ cup (4 ounces/1 stick) butter
- 4 large garlic cloves, chopped
- Grated zest of 1 large orange
- Juice of 1 large orange (about ⅓ cup)
- ¼ cup dry white vermouth
- ¼ cup chopped fresh basil leaves
- 1 cup dried apricots, thinly sliced
- Salt
- Lots of freshly ground black pepper
- ¼ cup finely chopped fresh parsley
- ¼ cup freshly grated Parmesan cheese

MELT BUTTER in a medium, noncorrosive skillet. Add garlic and orange zest and cook for 2 minutes. Stir in orange juice and vermouth, and simmer for 5 minutes.

Add basil, apricots, salt, and pepper, and cook another 3 minutes, or until slightly thickened. Immediately remove from heat or it will thicken too much. Stir in parsley and toss with hot pasta in a serving bowl. Sprinkle with Parmesan cheese and serve right away.

Pass extra grated cheese and the pepper mill for each person to add to taste. Serves 4.

Recommended Pasta: ¾ pound linguine or spaghetti

BROCCOLI BLUE CHEESE SAUCE

1 bunch broccoli, tough stems removed and broken into small flowerets
½ cup (4 ounces/1 stick) butter
4 large garlic cloves, chopped
2 large whole green onions, finely chopped
½ cup heavy or whipping cream
Salt
Lots of freshly ground black pepper
¼ pound blue cheese, crumbled
¼ cup freshly grated Parmesan cheese

STEAM BROCCOLI until just tender, then chop. You should have about 2¼ cups.

Melt butter in a large skillet. Add garlic, green onions, and broccoli, and sauté for 3 minutes. Stir in cream, salt, and pepper, and cook at a gentle boil until sauce thickens slightly.

Toss with hot pasta in a serving bowl. Add blue cheese and toss to distribute evenly. Add Parmesan cheese and toss again. Serve immediately.

Pass extra grated cheese and the pepper mill for each person to add to taste. Serves 4.

Recommended Pasta: ¾ pound fresh fettuccine

Broccoli and blue cheese are an exquisite combination. ♦ *If you are not a blue cheese fan you may omit it, but I have served this dish to many guests who say they dislike blue-veined cheeses and have received raves every time.*

A humble sauce; very rustic and earthy.

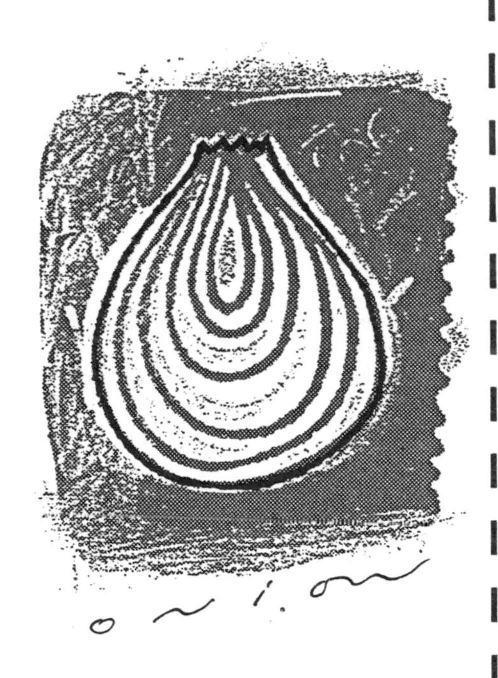

CHICKPEA SAUCE

- ¼ cup (2 ounces/½ stick) butter
- ¼ cup best-quality olive oil
- 1 medium onion, finely chopped
- 3 large garlic cloves, chopped
- 1 teaspoon dried rosemary
- 19-ounce (540-g) can chickpeas, undrained
- 2 tablespoons tomato paste
- 1 teaspoon salt
- Lots of freshly ground black pepper

MELT BUTTER with the oil in a medium skillet. Ada onion, garlic, and rosemary, and cook until onion is tender, about 3 minutes. Add remaining ingredients and simmer for about 10 minutes. Remove about 1 cup of the chickpea mixture to a food processor and purée. Return mixture to skillet, stir to combine and heat through. Do not continue to cook or it will thicken too much.

Toss with hot pasta in a serving bowl and serve at once. Serves 4.

Recommended Pasta: ¾ pound spaghetti or linguine

WHITE BEAN SAUCE

⅓ cup best-quality olive oil
4 large garlic cloves, finely chopped
¼ teaspoon hot red pepper flakes
1 rib celery, finely chopped
19-ounce (540-mL) can cannellini (white kidney) beans, drained
1 large ripe tomato (½ pound), cut into 1-inch cubes
1 teaspoon dried basil
¼ cup finely chopped fresh parsley
Salt
Lots of freshly ground black pepper

HEAT OIL in a large skillet. Add garlic, red pepper flakes, and celery, and cook until celery is tender, about 4 minutes.

Add beans, tomato, basil, parsley, salt, and pepper, and cook for 5 minutes or until slightly thickened. Toss with hot pasta and serve at once.

Pass extra grated cheese and the pepper mill for each person to add to taste. Serves 4.

Recommended Pasta: ½ pound penne, ziti, or rigatoni

Of the many sauces I've tasted, this remains one of my favorites. It is hearty, unrefined, and gloriously good served with a simple green salad and a strong red wine.

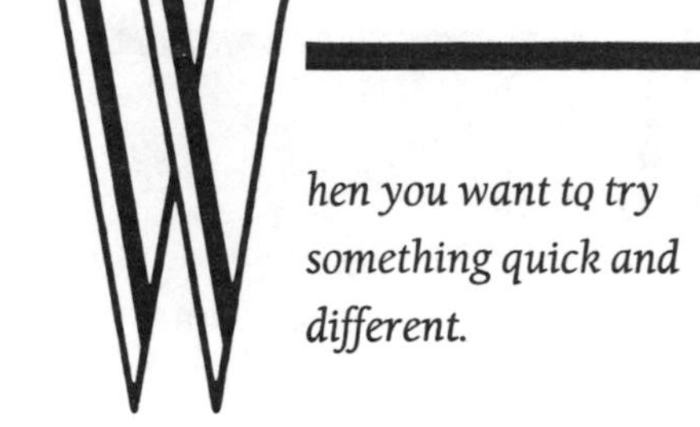

hen you want to try something quick and different.

Creamy Marinated Artichoke Sauce

¼ cup (2 ounces/½ stick) butter
4 large garlic cloves, finely chopped
6-ounce (170-mL) jar marinated artichoke hearts, drained, tough outer pieces removed, and chopped
1 teaspoon dried basil
¼ teaspoon cayenne
Salt
Lots of freshly ground black pepper
⅔ cup heavy or whipping cream
2 tablespoons freshly grated Parmesan cheese
2 tablespoons finely chopped fresh parsley, plus 2 tablespoons for garnish

MELT BUTTER in a medium skillet. Add garlic and cook for 1 minute. Stir in everything except cheese and parsley and cook at a gentle boil until sauce thickens slightly. Add Parmesan cheese and parsley, stir to mix, and toss with hot pasta in a serving bowl. Garnish with parsley and serve.

Pass extra grated cheese and the pepper mill for each person to add to taste. Serves 4.

Recommended Pasta: ¾ pound spaghettini, or linguine

LEMON CHIVE SAUCE

- ¼ cup (2 ounces/½ stick) butter
- 4 large garlic cloves, finely chopped
- 1 cup heavy or whipping cream
- Finely grated zest of 1 large lemon
- ⅓ cup freshly grated Parmesan cheese
- ¼ cup finely chopped fresh chives
- ¼ teaspoon freshly grated nutmeg
- 2 teaspoons fresh lemon juice
- Salt
- Lots of freshly ground black pepper

MELT BUTTER in a medium, noncorrosive skillet. Add garlic and cook for 1 minute. Stir in cream and lemon zest and cook at a gentle boil until sauce thickens slightly. Stir in cheese, chives, nutmeg, lemon juice, salt, and pepper. Toss with hot pasta and serve at once.

Pass extra grated cheese and the pepper mill for each person to add to taste. Serves 4.

Recommended Pasta: ½ pound penne

Lemon and chives make a delicious partnership. ♦ *If you happen to have some caviar in your larder (don't we all!), a dollop of it on top of each serving will complement the richness of the sauce.*

Slow-cooked onions attain a naturally sweet flavor, yet sugar is added to the sauce to sweeten it even more. ♦ If you are partial to onions, this might be just your thing.

Braised Onion Sauce

½ pound (2 sticks) butter
7 medium onions (1½ pounds), thinly sliced
1 tablespoon sugar
Salt
Lots of freshly ground black pepper
2 tablespoons dry white vermouth
½ cup finely chopped fresh parsley
Grated Parmesan cheese

MELT BUTTER in a medium, heavy skillet. Add onions, sugar, salt, and pepper, and sauté until onions are tender, about 5 minutes. Reduce heat to low, cover, and cook for 25 minutes, lifting lid occasionally to stir. The onions should be light golden and a very soft fragrant mass.

Stir in vermouth, turn heat to high, and cook 2 minutes, or until slightly thickened. Stir in parsley and toss with hot pasta in a serving bowl. Allow the pasta to sit for 3 to 4 minutes before serving to allow the flavor to develop.

Pass grated Parmesan cheese for each person to sprinkle to taste. Serves 4.

Recommended Pasta: ¾ pound linguine, spaghetti, or farfalle

Eggplant Tomato Sauce

1 pound eggplant, peeled and cut into 1-inch cubes
1 tablespoon salt
⅓ cup best-quality olive oil (or more if necessary)
1 medium onion, chopped
4 large garlic cloves, chopped
28-ounce (796-mL) can tomatoes, undrained
½ cup dry red wine
½ teaspoon dried thyme
1 teaspoon dried oregano
½ teaspoon salt
½ teaspoon freshly ground black pepper
½ cup finely chopped fresh parsley, plus ¼ cup for garnish
¼ cup capers, drained
15 Greek olives (Kalamata), pitted and chopped
Grated Parmesan cheese

PLACE EGGPLANT cubes in a colander, sprinkle with salt, and toss to coat evenly. Allow to drain for 30 minutes, rinse under cold running water, and dry well with a clean dish towel.

Heat oil in a large, heavy, noncorrosive skillet. Add eggplant, onion, and garlic, and sauté until eggplant is completely tender, about 15 minutes. Add remaining ingredients except capers, olives, and cheese, and simmer 20 minutes, or until sauce thickens slightly. Toss with hot pasta in a serving bowl, garnish with capers, olives, and parsley, and toss again at the table.

Pass grated Parmesan cheese for each person to sprinkle to taste. Serves 4.

Recommended Pasta: ½ pound penne or rigatoni

ggplant, tomatoes, capers, and olives give their essence to this hearty sauce. Delicious!

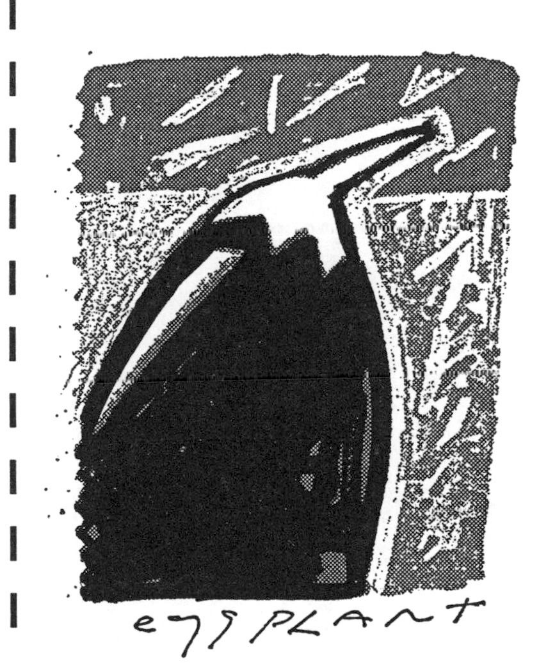

I like to serve this sauce over rotelle pasta (little wheels). ♦ It is a charming and light first course or main dish certain to delight hearts of palm devotees.

Hearts of Palm Sauce

½ cup (4 ounces/1 stick) butter
1 small onion, finely chopped
2 tablespoons dry white vermouth
¼ cup chicken broth
1 teaspoon dried basil
¼ cup finely chopped fresh chives
14-ounce (398-mL) can hearts of palm, drained and sliced into ¼-inch slices
Salt
Lots of freshly ground black pepper
4 sun-dried tomatoes in oil, drained and cut into julienne
¼ cup freshly grated Parmesan cheese

MELT HALF THE BUTTER in a medium skillet. Add onion and cook until tender, about 4 minutes. Stir in vermouth, turn heat to high, and cook until almost evaporated, about 4 minutes. Stir in chicken broth and cook until slightly thickened, about 3 minutes. Stir in remaining butter, basil, chives, hearts of palm, salt, and pepper. Cook until heated through, about 4 minutes.

Toss with hot pasta in a serving bowl and garnish with sun-dried tomatoes and Parmesan cheese. Serves 4.

Recommended Pasta: ½ pound rotelle, conchiglie, or fusilli

Swiss Chard Sauce

¼ cup best-quality olive oil
4 large garlic cloves, chopped
4 flat anchovy fillets, drained and minced
¼ teaspoon hot red pepper flakes, or to taste
1 large bunch Swiss chard (about 1½ pounds), stems removed, washed well, and chopped
¼ cup freshly grated Parmesan cheese

HEAT OIL in a medium skillet. Add remaining ingredients except Parmesan cheese and cook 5 minutes, or until garlic is tender and greens are wilted. The sauce will be soupy. Combine with hot pasta, sprinkle on cheese, and serve.

Pass extra grated cheese for each person to sprinkle to taste. Serves 4.

Recommended Pasta: ¾ pound orecchiette

Strong Mediterranean affinities are needed to enjoy this sauce, which is pungent with garlic, anchovies, and greens. Use orecchiette pasta (little ears) to catch the sauce. ♦ *Serve it in wide bowls along with some crusty bread to dunk in the sauce.*

Grill the summer squash first to bring out its delicate flavor, if you wish. But remember to reduce the cooking time, if you do.

Summer Squash and Basil Sauce

- ½ cup (4 ounces/1 stick) butter
- 4 medium yellow summer squash (1½ pounds), sliced then quartered
- 4 large garlic cloves, chopped
- ¼ teaspoon hot red pepper flakes, or to taste
- 3 whole green onions, finely chopped
- 1 cup chopped fresh basil leaves
- ½ cup finely chopped fresh parsley
- Salt
- Lots of freshly ground black pepper
- 3 tablespoons freshly grated Parmesan cheese

MELT BUTTER in a large, heavy skillet. Add squash and cook for 5 minutes. Add garlic and red pepper flakes, and cook 5 minutes longer, or until squash is cooked through. Stir in green onions, basil, parsley, salt, and pepper, and cook another 3 minutes. Toss with hot pasta, add Parmesan cheese, and toss again.

Pass extra grated cheese and the pepper mill for each person to add to taste. Serves 2 to 4.

Recommended Pasta: ½ pound penne or ziti

PRIMAVERA SAUCE

- ¼ cup (2 ounces/½ stick) butter
- 6 large garlic cloves, thinly sliced
- ¾ pound fresh peas, shelled (about ¾ cup)
- 1 sweet red pepper, cut into julienne
- 24 asparagus tips
- ½ cup finely chopped fresh parsley
- 1 large ripe tomato (½ pound), cut into 1-inch cubes
- ⅔ cup heavy or whipping cream
- Salt
- Lots of freshly ground black pepper
- 3 tablespoons freshly grated Parmesan cheese
- 1 teaspoon dried tarragon

MELT BUTTER in a large, heavy skillet. Add garlic, peas, red pepper, and asparagus tips, and sauté 5 minutes, or until vegetables are crisply tender.

Stir in parsley and tomato and cook another 5 minutes.

Add cream, salt, and pepper and cook at a gentle boil until sauce thickens slightly. Stir in Parmesan cheese and tarragon and serve over hot pasta.

Serve with or without extra grated cheese. Serves 2 to 4.

Recommended Pasta: ½ pound linguine or spaghetti

Primavera means "spring" in Italian, but I have seen many primavera sauces made with winter vegetables such as broccoli and cauliflower. Use whatever vegetables you like — the freshest ones you can find. ♦ I think the following combination is particularly flavorful and visually striking.

A spectacular-looking sauce that tastes as good as it looks. ♦ I use sweet red and yellow peppers rather than green peppers because of their intense sweetness and brilliant colors.

SWEET PEPPERS AND PINE NUT SAUCE

⅓ cup best-quality olive oil
4 large garlic cloves, chopped
2 sweet yellow peppers, seeded and cut into julienne
2 sweet red peppers, seeded and cut into julienne
½ cup pine nuts
1 tablespoon dried basil
½ cup finely chopped fresh parsley, plus 2 tablespoons for garnish
20 Greek olives (Kalamata), pitted and chopped
⅓ cup capers, drained
Salt
Lots of freshly ground black pepper

HEAT OIL in a large, heavy skillet. Add garlic and peppers and cook, stirring constantly, for 10 minutes.

Add pine nuts and cook another 5 minutes, or until golden colored. Sprinkle in basil and parsley, stir to mix, then add olives, capers, salt, and pepper. Toss with hot pasta in a serving bowl and garnish with parsley. Serves 4 to 6.

Recommended Pasta: ¾ pound penne or rigatoni

OYSTER MUSHROOM SAUCE

ich and earthy with a delightful woodsy taste, this sauce is ultimate bliss for mushroom lovers.

½ cup (4 ounces/1 stick) butter
1 pound fresh oyster mushrooms, wiped clean, and sliced into ½-inch pieces
⅓ cup finely chopped fresh parsley
Salt
Lots of freshly ground black pepper
⅔ cup heavy or whipping cream
4 whole green onions, finely chopped
¼ cup freshly grated Parmesan cheese

MELT BUTTER in a large, heavy skillet. Add mushrooms and cook until tender and lightly browned, about 5 minutes. Stir in parsley, salt, and pepper, and cook for another minute.

Pour in cream and cook at a gentle boil until sauce thickens slightly. Toss with hot pasta in a serving bowl, add chopped green onions and Parmesan cheese, and toss again. Serve immediately.

Pass extra grated cheese and the pepper mill for each person to add to taste. Serves 4.

Recommended Pasta: ¾ pound linguine or spaghetti

Fresh chanterelles, morels, and either oyster or shiitake mushrooms are the combination I prefer, but you may use any combination you like.

Wild Mushroom Sauce

½ cup (4 ounces/1 stick) butter
4 large garlic cloves, chopped
1 small onion, finely chopped
1 pound wild mushrooms, wiped clean, stems removed, and thinly sliced
½ cup heavy or whipping cream
1 teaspoon dried thyme
2 teaspoons dried tarragon

MELT BUTTER in a large, heavy skillet. Add garlic and onion and cook 3 minutes. Add mushrooms and sauté for 5 minutes, stirring constantly, or until mushrooms and onions are tender. Turn off heat, add cream and herbs, and stir to mix. Cream should thicken slightly on standing, but if it doesn't, turn heat on until thickened. Combine with hot pasta and serve.

No cheese with this sauce, please. Serves 4.

Recommended Pasta: ¾ pound fresh fettuccine

Creamy Mushroom with Orange Zest

- ¼ cup (2 ounces/½ stick) butter
- 4 large garlic cloves, finely chopped
- 1 pound mushrooms, wiped clean, and thinly sliced
- ½ teaspoon hot red pepper flakes, or to taste
- ½ cup finely chopped fresh parsley, plus 3 tablespoons for garnish
- 1 teaspoon dried basil
- Salt
- Lots of freshly ground black pepper
- ⅔ cup heavy or whipping cream
- Grated zest of 1 medium orange
- ¼ cup freshly grated Parmesan cheese

MELT BUTTER in a large, heavy skillet. Add garlic, mushrooms, red pepper flakes, parsley, basil, salt, and pepper, and sauté until the mushrooms give up their liquid and begin to brown.

Stir in the cream and cook at a gentle boil until sauce thickens slightly. Sprinkle in orange zest and Parmesan cheese. Combine with hot pasta and serve.

Pass extra grated cheese and the pepper mill for each person to add to taste. Serves 4 to 6.

Recommended Pasta: 1 pound linguine, spaghetti or fettuccine

Keep this sauce in mind when you want a dish that is simple and satisfying. ♦ The addition of orange zest turns an ordinary sauce into something very special.

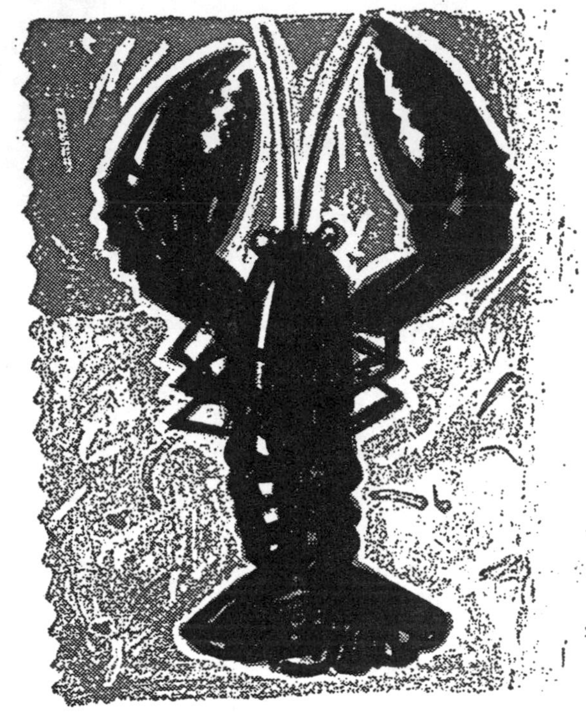

Lobster

SEAFOOD & FISH

SAUCES

♦ ♦ ♦

Glamorous enough for company, easy to make, and guaranteed to delight.

SMOKED SALMON IN CREAM SAUCE

- 2 tablespoons butter
- 1 large garlic clove, finely chopped
- 1 large whole green onion, finely chopped
- 6 ounces smoked salmon, trimmed, bones (if any) removed, and cut into julienne
- ¾ cup heavy or whipping cream
- ⅛ teaspoon freshly grated nutmeg
- ¼ teaspoon dried basil
- Lots of freshly ground black pepper
- 1 tablespoon freshly grated Parmesan cheese

MELT BUTTER in a medium skillet. Add garlic and green onion and cook for 1 minute. Add salmon and sauté for 2 minutes, then stir in cream, nutmeg, basil, and pepper. Cook at a gentle boil until sauce thickens slightly. Stir in Parmesan cheese and serve over hot pasta.

Pass extra grated cheese and the pepper mill for each person to add to taste. Serves 2 to 4.

Recommended Pasta: ½ pound linguine, spaghetti, or fettuccine

Anchovy, Lemon, and Parsley Sauce

¼ cup (2 ounces/½ stick) butter
¼ cup best-quality olive oil
8 to 10 anchovy fillets, drained and minced
6 large garlic cloves, chopped
¼ cup finely chopped fresh parsley, plus 2 tablespoons for garnish
Lots of freshly ground black pepper
1 tablespoon fresh lemon juice
¼ cup freshly grated Parmesan cheese

MELT BUTTER with the oil in a small, heavy skillet. Stir in everything except lemon juice and Parmesan cheese and cook for 3 minutes. Stir in lemon juice, cook for another 2 minutes, and toss with hot pasta in a serving bowl. Add Parmesan cheese, toss again, and garnish with parsley. Serve at once.

Extra freshly grated Parmesan cheese may be served as an accompaniment if desired. Serves 3 to 4.

Recommended Pasta: ¾ pound capellini, linguine, or spaghetti

A lot of people are not fond of anchovies, so don't tell them they are in this sauce – they may never know! ♦ *Anchovies, garlic, parsley, and lemon are a wonderful combination that never fails to delight those who appreciate down-to-earth flavors.*

I'm not ordinarily enamored of canned tuna, but I think it is delectable in this tangy sauce. ♦ For best results, use chunk light or solid white tuna and break it up into ½-inch to 1-inch pieces.

Tuna, Lemon, Caper, and Olive Sauce

½ cup (4 ounces/1 stick) butter
1 tablespoon best-quality olive oil
4 large garlic cloves, chopped
Finely grated zest of 1 large lemon
¼ cup fresh lemon juice
3 large whole green onions, finely chopped
2 tablespoons capers, drained
10 Greek olives (Kalamata), pitted and chopped
6½-ounce (184-g) can chunk light or solid white (not flaked) tuna, drained
Lots of freshly ground black pepper
Salt
¼ cup finely chopped fresh parsley

MELT BUTTER with oil in a small, noncorrosive, skillet. Add garlic and cook for 2 minutes. Add lemon zest, lemon juice, green onions, capers, and olives and cook another 2 minutes.

Turn heat to lowest setting. Add tuna and separate it (do not flake) with a fork into large pieces. Heat through, stirring very gently, being careful to keep the tuna in large chunks. Grind in pepper, sprinkle in salt, and taste for seasoning. Toss with hot pasta in a serving bowl, add parsley, and toss again.

Serve with or without grated Parmesan cheese. Serves 4.

Recommended Pasta: ½ pound penne or rigatoni

Clam Sauce

½ cup (4 ounces/1 stick) butter
4 large garlic cloves, chopped
2 large whole green onions, finely chopped
½ cup finely chopped parsley, plus 2 tablespoons for garnish
2 cans (5-ounces/142-g each) clams, drained, reserving ¼ cup broth
¼ cup dry white vermouth
Salt
Lots of freshly ground black pepper
1 tablespoon butter

MELT BUTTER in medium skillet. Add garlic, green onions, and parsley, and cook for 3 minutes. Stir in clam broth, vermouth, salt, and pepper, and cook for 4 minutes, or until liquid is reduced by half. Add clams and cook another minute. Toss immediately with hot pasta, add remaining butter, and toss again until melted. Garnish with parsley and serve. Serves 4.

Recommended Pasta: ¾ pound linguine or spaghetti

Canned clams, fresh parsley, and green onions join together in this savory sauce. ♦ Do not serve cheese with this sauce, please.

Unbelievably delicious. ♦ If you cannot obtain live littleneck clams that are no larger than two inches across, then I suggest you cook one of the other clam sauces instead. ♦ This sauce is somewhat soupy, so serve it in wide shallow bowls.

Steamed Clams and Garlic Sauce

- 3½ dozen littleneck clams
- ½ cup (4 ounces/1 stick) butter
- 6 large garlic cloves, chopped
- 1 small onion, finely chopped
- 1 bay leaf, broken in half
- 1 teaspoon dried thyme
- ¼ cup dry white vermouth
- Salt
- Lots of freshly ground black pepper
- ½ cup finely chopped fresh parsley, plus 2 tablespoons for garnish

CLEAN CLAMS by scrubbing each one and rinsing well under cold running water.

Melt half the butter in a heavy saucepan large enough to accommodate clams. Add garlic and onion and cook until tender, about 4 minutes. Add bay leaf, thyme, vermouth, salt, pepper, and clams. Cover and cook on moderate heat until clams open. Remove opened clams to a serving bowl with a slotted spoon. Discard any that do not open.

Add remaining butter and parsley to saucepan and cook for a minute or until butter is melted. Add drained pasta to serving bowl with clams and pour sauce over top. Toss thoroughly but gently and serve at once.

No cheese with this sauce, please. Serves 4.

Recommended Pasta: ¾ pound spaghetti or linguine

Crispy Bacon and Clam Sauce

10 slices bacon
1 tablespoon best-quality olive oil
1 small onion, finely chopped
4 large garlic cloves, chopped
½ cup finely chopped fresh parsley
½ teaspoon hot red pepper flakes, or to taste
½ teaspoon freshly ground black pepper
Salt
5-ounce (142-g) can clams, drained, reserving ¼ cup broth
Grated Parmesan cheese

In a large heavy skillet, fry bacon until crisp. Remove to a paper-towel-lined plate to drain. Pour bacon drippings into a small bowl, measure out ¼ cup, and discard the rest. Break bacon into bite-size pieces and set aside.

Pour reserved bacon drippings back into skillet. Add oil, onion, and garlic, and cook until tender, about 3 minutes. Add parsley, red pepper flakes, pepper, and salt, and cook for 2 minutes. Stir in clams and broth and cook until heated through. Combine with hot pasta, top with bacon pieces, and toss again at the table to mix in bacon.

Pass grated Parmesan cheese, if desired, and the pepper mill for each person to add to taste. Serves 4 to 6.

Recommended Pasta: ¾ pound linguine or spaghetti

Bacon and clams are an alluring combination. ♦ *Use good-quality bacon and do not toss it with pasta until just before serving to retain crispness.*

Mussels, wine, garlic, and tomatoes in a savory sauce is marvelous over pasta. ♦ The mussels must first be cleaned and bearded, which isn't difficult, just a little time-consuming.

Mussel Sauce

30 large mussels
½ cup (4 ounces/1 stick) butter
6 large garlic cloves, chopped
1 small onion, finely chopped
3 large sprigs parsley
1 bay leaf, broken in half
½ teaspoon hot red pepper flakes, or to taste
1 teaspoon dried thyme
¼ cup dry white vermouth
¼ cup chicken broth
½ cup chopped fresh parsley, plus 2 tablespoons for garnish
6 medium ripe tomatoes (2 pounds), chopped
2 teaspoons dried basil
Salt
Lots of freshly ground black pepper

CLEAN THE MUSSELS by scrubbing each one, pulling off the "beard" and rinsing well under cold running water.

Melt half the butter in a heavy saucepan large enough to accommodate mussels. Add garlic and onion and cook until tender, about 4 minutes. Add parsley sprigs, bay leaf, red pepper flakes, thyme, vermouth, chicken broth, and mussels. Cover and cook on moderate heat until all the shells are opened.

Remove opened mussels with a slotted spoon to a serving bowl. Discard any that do not open. Add parsley, tomatoes, basil, salt, pepper, and remaining butter to saucepan. Cook until sauce thickens slightly, about 5 to 10 minutes. Put mussels back into sauce and cook until heated through, about 3 minutes. Toss thoroughly but gently with hot pasta, garnish with parsley, and serve immediately.

No cheese with this sauce, please. Serves 4.

Recommended Pasta: ¾ pound linguine or spaghetti

HERBS, LEMON, AND SHRIMP SAUCE

½ cup (4 ounces/1 stick) butter
Grated zest of 1 large lemon
6 large garlic cloves, chopped
½ teaspoon hot red pepper flakes
2 teaspoons dried basil
2 teaspoons dried oregano
1 pound medium shrimp, shelled and deveined
½ cup finely chopped fresh parsley
2 whole green onions, finely chopped
Salt
Lots of freshly ground black pepper
¼ cup fresh lemon juice
¼ cup freshly grated Parmesan cheese

MELT BUTTER in a large, heavy skillet. Add lemon zest, garlic, red pepper flakes, basil, and oregano, and cook 2 minutes. Add shrimp and sauté until opaque, about 4 minutes. Add parsley, green onions, salt, and pepper, and cook 1 minute. Stir in lemon juice and cook another minute, then toss with hot pasta and Parmesan cheese, and serve at once.

Serve with or without extra grated cheese. Serves 4.

Recommended Pasta: ¾ pound spaghetti or linguine

This aromatic sauce is devastatingly delicious. So all you shrimp lovers, this one's for you!

Curry enthusiasts will love this sublime sauce. ♦ Take care not to overcook the shrimp and crabmeat.

Curried Shrimp and Crab Sauce

½ cup (4 ounces/1 stick) butter
4 large garlic cloves, chopped
1 small onion, finely chopped
½ cup chopped fresh parsley, plus 3 tablespoons for garnish
3 teaspoons good-quality curry powder, or to taste
¾ pound medium shrimp, shelled and deveined
½ pound fresh or frozen crabmeat, drained and squeezed dry
1 cup heavy or whipping cream
Salt
Lots of freshly ground black pepper
2 tablespoons freshly grated Parmesan cheese

MELT BUTTER in a large, heavy skillet. Add garlic, onion, and parsley, and cook until onion is tender, about 4 minutes. Stir in curry powder.

Add shrimp and crabmeat and stir to heat through, about 4 minutes. Add remaining ingredients and cook at a gentle boil until sauce thickens slightly.

Before saucing, carefully drain the pasta shells by shaking the strainer to remove excess water, or the sauce will be ruined. Toss the sauce with hot pasta in a serving bowl and garnish with parsley. Serve immediately. Serves 4.

Recommended Pasta: ¾ pound conchiglie, rotelle, or fusilli

Squid and Tomato Fennel Sauce

¼ cup best-quality olive oil
4 large garlic cloves, chopped
Small bulb fennel, tops removed and discarded, and chopped
1 shallot, chopped
1½ pounds squid, cleaned, sliced into rings, and tentacles cut in half if large
28-ounce (796-mL) can tomatoes, undrained
½ teaspoon salt
Lots of freshly ground black pepper
½ cup finely chopped fresh parsley
2 whole green onions, finely chopped
Grated Parmesan cheese

HEAT OIL in a large, noncorrosive skillet. Add garlic, fennel, and shallot and cook for 2 minutes. Add squid and cook until they turn opaque, about 3 minutes. Add tomatoes and liquid, salt, and pepper, and simmer until slightly thickened, about 30 minutes.

Just before pasta is cooked, add parsley and green onions to skillet, stir to mix, and toss with hot pasta in a serving bowl. Serve immediately.

Freshly grated Parmesan cheese may be served as an accompaniment if desired. Serves 4.

Recommended Pasta: ½ pound penne or rigatoni

The subtle licorice flavor of fennel with squid and tomatoes is an interesting alliance. ♦ Instructions for cleaning squid are in the glossary of ingredients. ♦ Italians never serve cheese with seafood, but I like it with this sauce.

This is a wonderfully luxurious sauce as long as you don't stint on the lobster. ♦ *Try to get female lobsters and add the red coral to the sauce — it contributes a luscious, subtle flavor.*

LOBSTER TARRAGON SAUCE

- 3 to 4 pounds (1 to 1½ pounds each) live lobsters, preferably female
- ½ cup (4 ounces/1 stick) butter
- 2 tablespoons dried tarragon
- Salt
- Lots of freshly ground black pepper
- Fresh lemon juice, to taste

COOK LOBSTERS in boiling, salted water for 10 minutes, or until cooked through. Cool and remove lobster meat and cut into bite-size pieces (there should be about 3 to 4 cups). Remove the coral, if any, and set aside.

Melt butter in a large, heavy skillet. Stir in tarragon, salt, pepper, and lobster meat. Cook until lobster is heated through, about 4 minutes. Stir in coral, if using, and add a bit of lemon juice, to taste. Serve over hot pasta.

No cheese with this sauce, please. Serves 4.

Recommended Pasta: ¾ pound capellini, linguine, or spaghetti

MEAT & POULTRY

SAUCES

♦ ♦ ♦

It is essential to use excellent-quality Italian sausages for this zesty sauce because the sausage flavors the oil which flavors the pasta. I like to use a combination of hot and mild sausages, but all hot or all mild works equally well.

♦ *Also, I don't remove the sausage casings because I like their chewy texture, but do remove them if you prefer.*

SPICY HOT ITALIAN SAUSAGE SAUCE

¼ cup best-quality olive oil (or more if necessary)
6 Italian sausages (about 1½ pounds), cut into ¼-inch thick slices
½ teaspoon hot red pepper flakes, or to taste
¾ cup finely chopped fresh parsley, plus 2 tablespoons for garnish
Salt
Lots of freshly ground black pepper
Grated Parmesan cheese

HEAT OIL in a large, heavy skillet. Add sausages and sauté until cooked through, about 5 minutes.

Add red pepper flakes, parsley, salt, and pepper, and cook another 2 minutes. Toss with hot pasta in a serving bowl and garnish with parsley.

Pass freshly grated Parmesan cheese for each person to add to taste. Serves 4.

Recommended Pasta: ¾ pound linguine

Creamy Prosciutto Olive Sauce

¼ cup (2 ounces/½ stick) butter
1 medium onion, finely chopped
2 large garlic cloves, finely chopped
¼ teaspoon hot red pepper flakes, or to taste
14 Greek olives (Kalamata), pitted and chopped
6 ounces thinly sliced prosciutto, cut into julienne
1 cup heavy or whipping cream
½ cup finely chopped fresh parsley, plus 2 tablespoons for garnish
1 large ripe tomato (½ pound), chopped
2 tablespoons freshly grated Parmesan cheese
Lots of freshly ground black pepper

MELT BUTTER in a medium skillet. Add onion, garlic, and red pepper flakes, and cook until tender, about 4 minutes. Add olives and prosciutto and cook until heated through. Stir in cream, parsley, tomato, cheese, and pepper, and cook at a gentle boil until sauce thickens slightly. Serve over hot pasta and garnish with parsley.

Pass extra grated cheese and the pepper mill for each person to add to taste. Serves 4.

Recommended Pasta: ½ pound penne

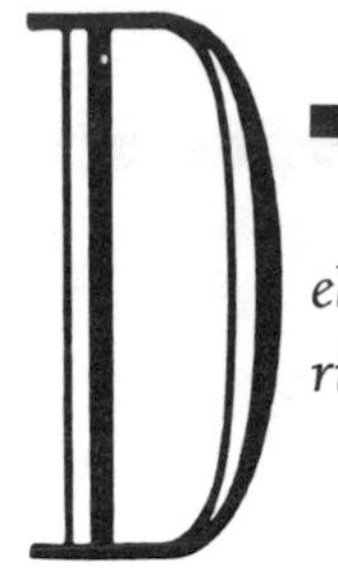

eliciously good and very rich.

At one time Americans thought this Italian-American specialty was Italy's national dish! Whether authentic or not, it can be wonderful when prepared with care. ♦ *Though normally paired with spaghetti, I prefer it with penne.*

Old-Fashioned Meatballs in Tomato Sauce

Meatballs:
½ pound ground pork
½ pound ground beef
¾ teaspoon freshly grated nutmeg
Salt
Lots of freshly ground black pepper
½ cup minced fresh parsley
½ teaspoon dried thyme
¼ cup freshly grated Parmesan cheese
1 egg
2 slices white bread, crusts removed and torn into small pieces (the size of green peas)

3 to 4 tablespoons olive oil

Sauce:
¼ cup (2 ounces/½ stick) butter
8 large garlic cloves, chopped
1 medium onion, chopped
28-ounce (796-mL) can tomatoes, undrained
5½-ounce (156-mL) can tomato paste
2 teaspoons dried basil
2 teaspoons dried oregano
6-inch cinnamon stick, broken in half
¼ teaspoon hot red pepper flakes
Salt
Lots of freshly ground black pepper
Grated Parmesan cheese

IN A LARGE BOWL, combine the meatball ingredients well (your hands work best) but do not handle it any more than you have to. Form the mixture into small meatballs about 1-inch in diameter. It yields approximately 40

Heat oil in a large skillet and fry in 2 batches until browned. Drain and set aside.

Melt butter in a medium, noncorrosive saucepan. Add garlic and onion and cook until onion is tender, about 4 minutes. Add remaining ingredients except cheese, lower heat, and simmer for 15 minutes. Add meatballs and simmer another 15 to 20 minutes, stirring occasionally. Serve over hot pasta.

Pass grated Parmesan cheese and the pepper mill for each person to add to taste. Serves 4.

Recommended Pasta: ½ pound penne or rigatoni

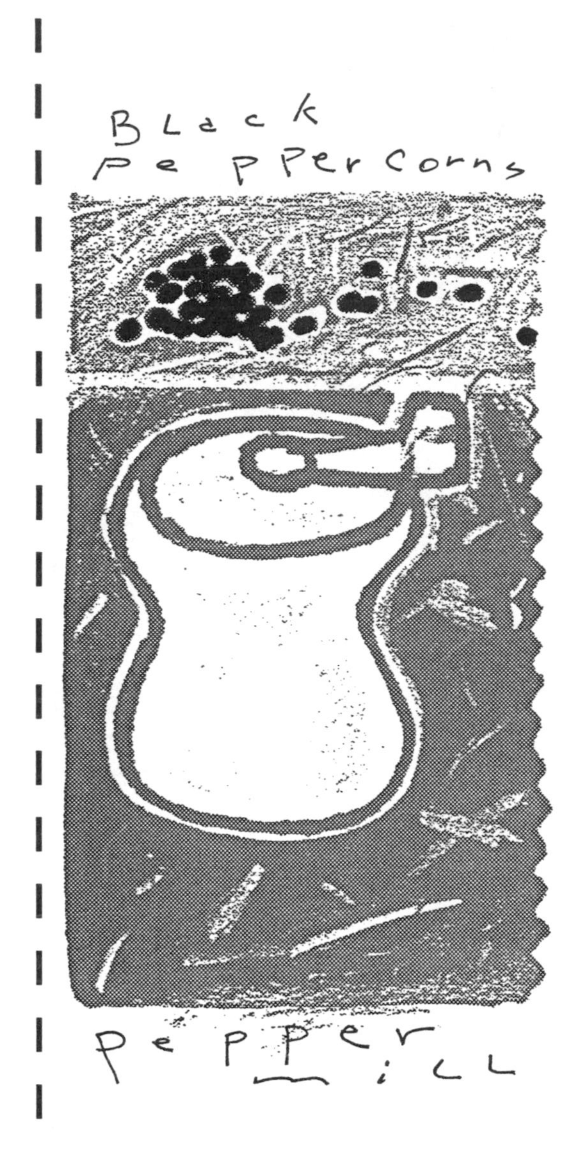

Chicken, Tarragon, and Tomato Sauce

A wonderful, French-inspired sauce, its flavor heightened by the fragrant perfume of tarragon.

¼ cup (2 ounces/½ stick) butter
3 boned chicken breast halves, skinned and cubed
3 large garlic cloves, chopped
1 small onion, finely chopped
3 medium ripe tomatoes (1 pound), seeded and chopped
2 tablespoons dried tarragon
1 tablespoon Canadian whisky
2 tablespoons dry white vermouth
¼ cup chicken broth
1 cup heavy or whipping cream
Salt
Lots of freshly ground black pepper
⅓ cup finely chopped fresh parsley, plus 2 tablespoons for garnish
Grated Parmesan cheese

MELT BUTTTER in a medium skillet. Add chicken and sauté until lightly browned, about 4 minutes. Remove chicken to a plate. Add garlic and onion to skillet, and cook until tender, about 3 minutes. Add tomatoes and tarragon, and cook for 3 minutes. Pour in whisky, vermouth, and chicken broth, and cook on high heat until reduced by about two-thirds. Stir in cream, salt, and pepper, and cook on high heat until sauce thickens slightly.

Lower heat and add cooked chicken. Simmer to heat through, about 3 minutes, stir in parsley, and taste for seasoning. Toss with hot pasta in a serving bowl, garnish with parsley, and serve at once.

Pass grated Parmesan cheese and the pepper mill for each person to add to taste. Serves 4.

Recommended Pasta: ¾ pound spaghettini or linguine

Chicken Artichoke Sauce

½ cup (4 ounces/1 stick) butter
6 large garlic cloves, chopped
1 pound mushrooms, wiped clean and thinly sliced
2 cans (14-ounces/398-mL each) artichoke hearts, drained and sliced
2 teaspoons dried basil
2 teaspoons dried oregano
¼ cup chicken broth
¼ cup dry white vermouth
1 cup heavy or whipping cream
2½- to 3-pound chicken, roasted, skinned, then meat removed and torn into large bite-size pieces
Salt
Lots of freshly ground black pepper
1 cup finely chopped fresh parsley

MELT BUTTER in a large, heavy skillet. Add garlic and mushrooms and sauté for 3 minutes. Add artichokes and cook another 3 minutes. Stir in basil, oregano, and chicken broth, and turn heat to high. Boil until broth is reduced somewhat, add vermouth, and continue boiling until reduced by two-thirds, about 5 minutes.

Add cream and reduce at a gentle boil until slightly thickened. Add chicken and heat through, stir in salt, pepper, and parsley, and toss with hot pasta. Serve at once.

Serve with or without grated Parmesan cheese. Serves 6 to 8.

Recommended Pasta: ¾ pound fusilli

An incredibly delectable sauce that is chock-full of mushrooms, artichoke hearts, and chicken. It is perfect company fare. ♦ The chicken may be roasted a day ahead.

ot very glamorous sounding, but it is delicious all the same.

Chicken Liver Sauce

- ¼ cup (2 ounces/½ stick) butter
- 3 tablespoons best-quality olive oil
- 2 large garlic cloves, chopped
- 1 small onion, finely chopped
- ¾ pound chicken livers, trimmed and roughly chopped
- ½ pound fresh mushrooms, wiped clean and chopped
- 1 teaspoon dried thyme
- ½ teaspoon hot red pepper flakes, or to taste
- ½ cup finely chopped fresh parsley, plus 2 tablespoons for garnish
- Salt
- Lots of freshly ground black pepper
- ¼ cup freshly grated Parmesan cheese

MELT BUTTER with the oil in a medium skillet. Add garlic and onion and cook for 2 minutes. Add chicken livers and sauté until lightly browned but still pink inside. Add mushrooms, thyme, red pepper flakes, parsley, salt, and pepper; sauté until mushrooms are tender, about 3 minutes. Toss with hot pasta in a serving bowl, add grated cheese and toss again. Garnish with parsley and serve.

Pass extra grated cheese and the pepper mill for each person to add to taste. Serves 4.

Recommended Pasta: ¾ pound spaghettini or linguine

Sweetbreads and Tomato Sauce

n irresistible, savory sauce. ♦ *If you have never tried sweetbreads, now is the time.*

- ¾ pound sweetbreads
- 1 teaspoon white vinegar
- ½ cup (4 ounces/1 stick) butter
- 6 ounces pancetta, diced
- 5 medium onions (1 pound), chopped
- 5 large garlic cloves, finely chopped
- 28-ounce (796-mL) can tomatoes, undrained
- 1 cup chopped fresh basil leaves, plus 2 tablespoons for garnish
- 1 teaspoon dried basil
- Lots of freshly ground black pepper
- ¼ cup (2 ounces/½ stick) butter
- Grated Parmesan cheese

Cover sweetbreads with cold water. Add vinegar and soak for 2 hours.

Place sweetbreads in a saucepan of boiling water; bring back to a boil and cook for 3 minutes. Plunge them into icewater, drain, and dry with paper towels. Peel off membrane and gristle and refrigerate until needed. This may be done a day in advance.

Slice sweetbreads into bite-size pieces and set aside.

Melt butter in a large skillet. Add pancetta, onions, and garlic, and cook until onions are tender, about 4 minutes. Add sweetbreads and cook another minute. Stir in tomatoes and liquid, the fresh and dried basil, and pepper, and cook 10 minutes, or until sauce thickens slightly. Add remaining butter, stir, and toss with hot pasta in a serving bowl. Garnish with basil.

Freshly grated Parmesan cheese may be served as an accompaniment if desired. Serves 4.

Recommended Pasta: ¾ pound fusilli

PASTA SALADS

♦ ♦ ♦

Slightly hot and spicy, this salad is simple to assemble. ♦ If you like, you can buy a quarter roast duck from a Chinese restaurant or barbecue shop, tear the meat into bite-size pieces, and add to the salad for a more substantial dish.

Oriental Noodles with Orange and Green Onion

- 1 tablespoon roughly chopped fresh ginger
- 1 medium garlic clove
- 1 tablespoon chili paste with soy bean
- 1 teaspoon soy sauce
- 1 teaspoon balsamic vinegar
- 4 teaspoons Oriental sesame oil
- 2 tablespoons peanut oil
- 1 tablespoon sugar
- ½ pound dried soba or buckwheat noodles, cooked and rinsed in cold water to cool
- 1 large orange, peeled, sectioned, and cut into 1-inch pieces
- 1 large green onion (green part only), finely chopped

IN A FOOD PROCESSOR, mince ginger and garlic. Add remaining ingredients except the noodles, orange, and green onion, and combine. Toss with the cold, well-drained noodles, add the orange, green onion, and duck pieces (if using), and toss again. Serves 2 to 4.

A gorgeous pasta salad for seafood lovers. ♦ Serve this as a first course, a luncheon entrée, or a light, summer main course along with some crusty French bread and a crisp white wine.

Fusilli with Seafood in Lemon Vinaigrette

Lemon Vinaigrette:
1 cup best-quality olive oil
Finely grated zest of 3 medium lemons
⅔ cup fresh lemon juice
½ teaspoon Dijon-style mustard
Salt
Lots of freshly ground black pepper

½ pound fusilli
1 pound medium shrimp, shelled and deveined
2 pounds squid, cleaned
½ pound fresh or frozen crabmeat, drained and squeezed dry
½ pound fresh peas, shelled (about ½ cup), uncooked
½ medium sweet red pepper, seeded and cut into ½-inch cubes
½ medium sweet yellow pepper, seeded and cut into ½-inch cubes
1 teaspoon dried basil
½ cup finely chopped fresh parsley, plus ¼ cup for garnish
Salt
Lots of freshly ground black pepper

COMBINE VINAIGRETTE ingredients in a bowl and set aside.

Bring a large pot of water to a rolling boil, add fusilli and cook until al dente. With a slotted spoon, remove pasta to a colander to drain and toss with a little vinaigrette to prevent sticking. Add shrimp to the same rapidly boiling water. Cook until opaque in the center, remove with a slotted spoon to drain, then place in a glass or ceramic bowl. Add pasta to bowl and set aside.

Slice the squid bodies into rings and cut the tentacles, if large. Drop into the same rapidly boiling water and cook for 1 minute if squid are small, or longer if very large. Test one for tenderness and continue cooking until tender, if necessary. Drain and add to the seafood and pasta in bowl.

Add remaining ingredients and half the vinaigrette to bowl. Mix thoroughly but gently and continue adding vinaigrette until ingredients are well coated. Adjust seasonings, cover, and let flavors blend for 30 minutes. Refrigerate if not serving right away. Garnish with parsley before serving. Serves 6 to 8.

Light and refreshing, this salad makes an engaging luncheon entrée, side dish, or a fine buffet dish.

Chicken or Turkey Pasta Salad with Apples, Orange Zest, and Currants

½ pound conchiglie, cooked, drained, and rinsed to cool with cold water
2 medium ribs celery, finely chopped (about ¾ cup)
4 Granny Smith apples, unpeeled, cored, and chopped
½ cup dried currants
Grated zest of 2 large oranges
4 cups cooked chicken or turkey, skinned and torn into large bite-size pieces
1 cup homemade or Hellman's mayonnaise
¾ cup natural, unflavored yogurt
Salt
Freshly ground black pepper

Combine ingredients in a noncorrosive bowl and refrigerate until ready to serve. Serves 6 to 8.

INDEX